Church
and
State

CHURCH AND STATE

*Government
and Religion
in the
United States*

Kathlyn Gay

Issue and Debate

*The Millbrook
Press*

*Brookfield,
Connecticut*

Photographs courtesy of: The Bettmann Archive: pp. 17, 22, 33, 50, 64, 67; Religious News Service: pp. 37, 41, 88; AP/Wide World Photos: pp. 56, 74; Wicks / The Signal / Rothco: p. 61; UPI/ Bettmann: pp. 68, 71, 77, 85, 90; Spencer Grant, Monkmeyer Press: p. 80; Kirk Condyles/Impact Visuals: p. 93; Americans United: p. 96; Illinois State Historical Society: p. 104.

Library of Congress Cataloging-in-Publication Data

Gay, Kathlyn.
Church and state : government and religion in the United States /
by Kathlyn Gay.
p.   cm.
Includes bibliographical references and index.
Summary: Discusses the division between government and religion
in the United States and problems in such areas as school prayer,
public displays of religious symbols, and religious practices that
violate the law.
ISBN 1-56294-063-5 (lib. bdg.)
1. Church and state—United States—Juvenile literature.
2. Religion in the public schools—United States—Juvenile
literature.   3. Religion and politics—United States—Juvenile
literature.   4. Freedom of religion—United States—Juvenile
literature.   [1. Church and state.   2. Freedom of religion.]
I. Title.
BR516.G37   1992
322'.1'0973—dc20   91-34753   CIP   AC

Contents

*Church
and
State*

One Nation Under Whose God?

If you were asked to name some of the freedoms Americans enjoy, you would probably list, along with free speech and a free press, religious freedom. Unlike countries in which governments support a state (that is, a national) religion—whether it be Christianity, Judaism, Hinduism, Islam, Buddhism, or another faith—in the United States the Constitution forbids an established religion. In fact, Americans expect government to stay out of religious affairs, and religion not to dominate government functions. But there has been and continues to be controversy over whether there should be rigid barriers between the sacred and the secular or whether religion should play some role in public life.

Consider these events:

■ A state supreme court rules that it is illegal to deny unemployment benefits to two Native American workers who were fired from their jobs for using the nonaddictive but illegal drug peyote in religious services. But the U.S.

Supreme Court—the nation's highest court—overturns the ruling, saying that the workers' religious practices were not exempt from state law, and the state can deny benefits when a person is fired for illegal activities.

- A federal judge orders U.S. immigration officials to stop spying on churches that provide safe havens for illegal immigrants who have fled abusive governments in other countries. (Because they have opposed their governments, the immigrants fear they will be killed by agents of those governments.)

- The U.S. Supreme Court upholds a law that allows both secular (nonreligious) and religious groups to conduct programs in high schools with the aim of convincing teenagers to abstain from premarital sex.

- U.S. Supreme Court justices declare that a city may display a menorah, a candelabrum that symbolizes the Jewish Chanukah festival, but prohibit the display of a Nativity scene during the Christmas season.

These cases highlight just a few of the conflicts that arise within the broad context of church-state issues, as they are usually called. Most of the questions and controversy about the roles of religion and government come about because there are different interpretations of the U.S. Constitution and federal and state laws. But other disputes arise over moral or ethical issues that are related to what is considered acceptable behavior in society. Thus church-state issues fit into three broad categories, or areas of conflict.

Areas of Conflict. Two areas of conflict involve the First Amendment to the U.S. Constitution. In brief, the First

Amendment says that the government cannot *establish* a religion—that is, promote, endorse, or identify itself with any particular religion or with religion in general. Questions about government establishment of religion are raised, for example, when a local government decides to place a Christmas Nativity scene (with obvious religious symbols) on government property.

The First Amendment also says that each of us is guaranteed *free exercise* of religion, which means the right to practice a religion or not practice a religion, according to one's own beliefs. In some cases the free exercise of religion may conflict with local, state, or federal laws, but people may be exempt from a law that compels them to violate their religious beliefs. For example, some religious groups believe that all armed conflict is sinful, and that their members should not serve in the armed forces, even if a federal draft law requires military service. The government may accommodate such religious views by waiving the requirement to join the military.

On the other hand, some religious practices may be restricted. A church in Kentucky, for example, was barred from using rattlesnakes and copperheads in religious services, even though church members claimed that they were following biblical instructions to "take up serpents." The practice was outlawed because it endangered the health and safety of citizens.

Besides the constitutional and legal questions raised in regard to church-state matters, there are also political and social issues. This third area of conflict usually focuses on whether a given religious practice is appropriate behavior and how religious traditions should be maintained. Such issues were raised in two recent cases in which Boy Scouts refused to pledge their duty to God. The pledge is part of the Scout Promise, but was contrary to the views of the Scouts' families, who were atheists (people who do not believe in God). The boys were expelled from their troops, and their parents sued the Boy Scouts of America for discriminatory practices.

Another example of this third type of conflict is the question of whether ministers, priests, and other members of the clergy should take part in political activities. The clergy are allowed by law to be active in political campaigns and to be candidates for political office. But some Americans worry about the way religious leaders' beliefs will affect political decisions or whether the clergy can live according to their conscience and still respect the diversity of religious views in the United States.

Early Ties Between Church and State. Conflicts over the role of religion in American life have occurred since Europeans first settled in North America during the 1600s. But the focus and vigor of the arguments have changed with the times.

To begin with, early settlers in the New World sought religious liberty, but they did not allow it for all. In the first English colony of Virginia, the founders set up an official Anglican (English) Church patterned after the Church of England, the main religious group in England. The various Protestants had established their own churches after breaking away from the Roman Catholic Church, which had united people of Christian faith throughout Europe during the Middle Ages. But the Church of England retained many of the rituals and practices of the Catholic Church. The king of England appointed church officials, and Parliament (the legislature) set laws mandating what people should believe and how they should worship.

The Virginia founders expected to develop a replica of a British community, including an established state (government-supported) church. All colonists, regardless of their religious beliefs, were taxed to pay for the building and maintenance of the Anglican Church, which later became known as the Protestant Episcopal, or simply Episcopal, Church. Laws also mandated that people attend church, and there were harsh penalties for those who did not abide by church teaching. Those groups who disagreed or wanted to practice their own beliefs were barred from the colony or chased out.

Not all British colonists wanted to maintain such close ties with the English church. Some settlers who founded colonies in North America had completely separated themselves from the Church of England, and thus were known as Separatists. Most Separatists believed that they should live by biblical laws, not those decreed by a king and a state church. When England's King James I threatened to force the Separatists from the land unless they accepted the Church of England, the dissenters tried to establish homes first in the Netherlands and then in the "New World." These Pilgrims, as Americans later described them, sailed on the *Mayflower* from England to North America to found the Plymouth colony in Massachusetts. They hoped to be completely free of a state-mandated church.

At first the Pilgrims allowed a fair amount of religious liberty in Plymouth colony. But they were soon influenced by other settlers, particularly Puritans, another well-known group of religious dissenters from England. The Puritans founded the Massachusetts Bay colony, which they expected to be "a heavenly city" governed by biblical codes. Rules covered not only church attendance but also clothing, the conduct of business, the education of children, and permissible types of recreation. Only members of the Congregational Church, the established religion, were allowed to vote, and membership in the church was limited to those whose beliefs and life-styles conformed to church doctrine.

In short, the Puritans believed that there should be close ties between religious and social practices and that the state (government) should accommodate itself to the church, or the will of God. The leaders of the Massachusetts Bay colony strictly enforced church rules and harassed and drove out Catholics and members of such Protestant groups as Baptists and Quakers. Certainly nonconformists like Thomas Morton were not welcome.

Morton was a British trader who bartered with Native Americans, offering liquor and guns for furs. Morton and his trading partners also celebrated ancient British games that included rowdy dances around a Maypole. To many settlers in Massachusetts and in other parts of New England, Morton's activities were sinful and a threat to their way of life. He was eventually arrested and exiled to England, where he wrote scathing criticisms of the colonists' religious bigotry.[1]

Massachusetts was not alone in its religious intolerance. Except for Rhode Island, Pennsylvania, and Delaware, all of the colonies, whether settled by the British, the Dutch, or other Europeans, set up state churches. For many settlers, the established church was a way to replicate part of the old world in the new; structures and institutions reminded colonists of their homelands. Whatever the established church, it also protected the interests of the majority, while oppressing those dissenters who might disrupt the social order.

An Act of Tolerance. As an increasing number of settlers with varying backgrounds arrived in North America, conditions slowly changed. For one thing, many more people who opposed the idea of an established church populated the land. Some settled in the colony of Maryland, which was founded by Cecilius Calvert, a Roman Catholic. Calvert named the colony in honor of Queen Henrietta

Religious nonconformity was not tolerated by the Puritans. Extreme forms of persecution, such as public whippings, were practiced against groups like the Quakers in an effort to drive them out of Massachusetts Bay colony.

Maria, the wife of England's King Charles I and also a Catholic.

Although Calvert remained in England, he and his family developed profitable business ventures in the Maryland colony. At the same time, the Calverts established the colony as a haven for Roman Catholics, who had long been persecuted in England and in other British colonies in the New World. Restrictions against Catholics relaxed somewhat after 1625, during the reign of Charles I, but English law required Catholics to attend religious services that conflicted with their beliefs.

In Maryland, those regulations no longer applied when the colonial assembly (a legislative body) passed the Maryland Toleration Act of 1649. The law allowed Catholics as well as some Protestant groups the freedom to worship as they chose. However, Unitarians, Jews, and any others who denied the doctrine of the Trinity (the three persons in one god) or that Jesus Christ was the son of God could be executed for expressing such views.

Although the Maryland colony was considered a tolerant community for its time, *tolerance* by definition (and usually in practice) means to put up with or endure. Tolerance assumes an attitude of superiority. The dominant group permits other groups certain privileges as long as the "inferior" groups do not have equal social and political status. Religious tolerance and religious freedom, then, are not synonymous.

But some settlements established during the colonial period went beyond mere tolerance to grant broader religious freedoms, thanks to the efforts of leaders like Roger Williams and William Penn. Both believed strongly in freedom of individual conscience and thought government should stay out of religious matters.

When Roger Williams disagreed with the Puritan leaders in the Massachusetts Bay colony and spoke out for freedom of individual conscience, he was banished from the colony. But in 1636, Williams bought a tract of land from Native Americans who lived along Narragansett Bay, and he began a settlement that later became known as Rhode Island.

Williams's settlement was a refuge for Jews, Quakers, and others who believed in religious liberty. However, there was discrimination against Catholics, who were allowed to settle in Rhode Island but were denied the right to vote. Nevertheless, Williams's ideas on religious freedom were influential in later years when the U.S. Constitution was drafted. Today, many historians consider Williams a champion of religious liberty and credit him with helping to spread the concept that government should be separated from religious affairs.

William Penn also was adamant about the right of every person to worship as he or she pleased. Penn originally belonged to the Church of England, but in his early twenties he left the established church to become a member of the Society of Friends, or Quakers, as they came to be called. Like other Quakers, Penn believed that God spoke to people through their conscience, and that people should not be forced to fight wars, pledge allegiance to a government, or show deference to royalty. Such respect, Quakers believed, belonged only to God.

Because they openly professed beliefs that seemed to threaten established authority, the Quakers were publicly whipped and often jailed. Penn, too, was jailed, but he continued to work for religious freedom and planned for a New World colony where no government would be allowed to rule over a person's conscience. The new colony of Pennsylvania eventually became the home of many diverse groups, including Anabaptists (now known as the Pennsylvania Dutch or Plain People) and people who professed no religious affiliation.

As religious leaders in the thirteen colonies were attempting to establish communities founded on the idea of religious liberty, some, like Penn, also maintained that people should be free to make their own laws and run their own government. Without civil liberties, religious freedom was not possible. Increasingly, this principle became more broadly accepted, particularly as scientists, philosophers, and others condemned absolute government and advocated free thought and free speech.

One of those who opposed the total control exercised by British royalty was Thomas Paine. Paine, who was born in England and moved to America, wrote a pamphlet called *Common Sense*, urging people to free themselves from the oppression of kings. Thousands of copies of the pamphlet were published and distributed throughout the colonies. Some historians believe the publication of Paine's pamphlet was one of the most important events leading to the colonists' Declaration of Independence from British rule in 1776.

2

A "Wall of Separation"

Not long before declaring independence, each of the soon-to-be states in America began to develop a written constitution, a legal framework for the way each government would function. Government had to be limited; it could not trample on inherent rights—those that should apply to all people. Virginia was the first state to adopt a constitution that included a declaration of rights, called "one of the great liberty documents of all time."[2] It did so on June 29, 1776, just a few days before the Continental Congress declared independence.

A First Step Toward Religious Freedom. Patrick Henry was one statesman who had a major role in framing the Virginia constitution. A young lawyer, Henry had often spoken out against unfair British taxation. Before the colonies declared their independence, Henry had urged the Virginia militia to arm themselves, declaring in what is now a well-known battle cry: "Give me liberty or give me death."

Known as an eloquent speaker, Virginia statesman Patrick Henry was among the first to argue in favor of the free exercise of religion.

Henry also defended Baptist ministers who were jailed for their religious practices. Many Virginians who belonged to the established Anglican church thought Baptists were fanatical. But Henry believed that all people "are equally entitled to the free exercise of religion, according to the dictates of conscience," as he stated in a Virginia bill, or proposed law, that he helped to write.[3]

Although Henry's bill did not become law, other statesmen also worked to bring about religious freedom in Virginia. Thomas Jefferson, who wrote the Declaration of Independence and later became the third U.S. president, wrote and helped pass laws in Virginia that prevented any church from being a state church.

One of the first acts abolished laws that required church attendance and repealed punishments for people who followed religious practices other than those of the established church. In addition, Virginians no longer had to support the established church with tax funds. Patrick Henry and many other Virginia citizens, however, were not against the idea of tax support for religion. Instead, they believed tax funds should be used to assist all Christian churches. Henry proposed a tax to help sustain "some form of Christian worship," which he believed would lead to high moral standards and generally benefit the social structure of the state.

But Jefferson and some other state leaders did not agree. Jefferson proposed instead a law called the Statute for Religious Freedom, which was designed to completely separate religion and government. His bill was introduced in 1779 but was not voted on until seven years later. It was presented for consideration by James Madison, Jefferson's friend and a legislator who long had argued for the right of every person to live by her or his own conscience.

Madison previously had convinced the legislature to vote down tax support for religious institutions. His arguments were presented in a petition called the *Memorial and Remonstrance against Religious Assessments.* To present his case, Madison declared that taxation to support the Christian religion was not necessary because "this religion both existed and flourished, not only without the support of human laws, but in spite of every opposition from them."[4]

His *Memorial* also argued that if the state supported Christianity in general, then it could at some time set up a particular denomination or sect as the state religion. And doing that, he argued, would in turn destroy harmony among the varied religious groups. Restricting religious freedom would endanger other liberties, such as freedom of speech and the press. Largely because of Madison's arguments, the Virginia legislature passed the Jefferson statute in 1786. Virginia became the first state to legally declare that the affairs of government and religion should be separate. The concepts that produced the Virginia Statute for Religious Freedom were also influential in shaping the First Amendment to the U.S. Constitution.[5]

Developing the Bill of Rights. When the U.S. Constitution was adopted in 1789, it included only a brief statement about religion. The last paragraph of Article VI states that government officials "shall be bound by Oath or Affirmation" to support the Constitution, "but no religious Test shall ever be required as a Qualification to any Office or public Trust under the United States."

Although the framers of the Constitution made no reference to religious or other individual freedoms, they believed these liberties were assured. Why? Because the framers had drafted a Constitution that limited the federal, or national, government's powers and allowed the states all the powers not clearly assigned to the federal government. The Constitution also provides for three branches of the federal government—the executive, the legislative, and the judicial. These divisions prevent any one branch from gaining too much power and allow each branch to take actions that counter those of another. Such checks and balances in the federal government were meant to be safeguards against tyranny.

However, many Americans were concerned because the Constitution did not specify civil and religious liberties assured to the people. State leaders were fearful that history would repeat itself and that one person or group within a strong national government would become powerful enough to oppress the ruled. Many state delegates who were to ratify, or approve, the U.S. Constitution would not sign unless there were amendments that protected individual liberties.

James Madison believed that a long list of specific rights was unnecessary and might even be used by would-be tyrants to limit freedoms. Nevertheless, he felt that amendments could address some of the most pressing public concerns about abuses of power. Madison prepared twelve amendments, ten of which were ratified as part of the Constitution in 1791. Known as the Bill of Rights, the amendments protect freedom of religion, of speech, and of the press, and other basic rights.

The First and the Fourteenth Amendments. The First Amendment to the U.S. Constitution guarantees religious liberty. It begins with the sentence, "Congress shall make no law respecting an establishment of religion, or prohibiting the free exercise thereof." The first clause of that sentence, often called the "establishment clause," makes it clear that Congress cannot pass a law to establish, or support, a state church—the federal government cannot favor one religion over another. The second clause provides for the free exercise of religion, or the freedom for a person to live according to her or his conscience or religious beliefs.

After the Bill of Rights was passed, some states changed their constitutions to provide for separation of church and state and religious liberty. But the Bill of Rights itself applied only to the federal government. It was not until the Fourteenth Amendment was passed after the Civil War that the Bill of Rights could be applied to the states.

The Fourteenth Amendment includes five sections, the first of which declares, in part, that no state can "deprive any person of life, liberty, or property, without due process of law; nor deny to any person within its jurisdiction the equal protection of the laws." Over the years, the U.S. Supreme Court has interpreted the Fourteenth Amendment to mean that state and local governments must adhere to the Constitution's Bill of Rights just as the federal government does.

A Wall or a Fence? The First Amendment (backed up by the Fourteenth) frequently has been referred to as a "wall of separation" between church and state, a phrase coined by Thomas Jefferson when he was president. Jefferson had been asked to proclaim a national day of fasting as a religious observance, but he refused, explaining in a letter that religion was a matter of individual conscience. He wrote that he had "sovereign reverence" for the U.S. Constitution—the law "of the whole American people"— and the First Amendment, which in his opinion had built "a wall of separation between church and State."[6]

Over the years, people have often used the metaphor of the wall to describe the meaning of the First Amendment. But that figure of speech has created many conflicts among American citizens and raised many legal arguments. Some have argued that "the wall must be kept high and impregnable," as Supreme Court Justice Hugo Black wrote in 1947. He was referring to a case known as *Everson* v. *Board of Education.* The case questioned the right of the state of New Jersey to use tax funds to bus children to both public and private (usually religious) schools.

In his majority ruling, Justice Black emphasized that the First Amendment prohibited the government from passing any laws that would promote or support with tax funds any or all religions. But in line with an earlier ruling, he declared that tax funds could be used to pay for the bus service because it was a matter of public safety—students would not have to walk along busy highways to get to school. Tax-supported health and welfare services were allowed for both sectarian (religious) and nonsectarian schools, and such services were not considered support for religious activities or institutions. In addition, the Court said the government was not taking a position that pitted the secular (nonreligious) against the religious. However, Justice Black said that the New Jersey law was at the limit of what the First Amendment allowed.[7]

Some experts today argue that the Everson case and many others since then on church-state issues show that there are cracks in the wall of separation. Others contend that there has never been a real wall at all. Instead, the partition between church and state may be more like a picket fence, as two philosophy professors suggested in an article on the separation issue. They believe their metaphor apt because

> *pickets can be added from time to time, thus strengthening the fence, or they can just about as easily be removed, thus weakening it. Historically, those inclined to add pickets are called strict separationists; those inclined to remove*

pickets, accommodationists. In recent decades both groups have busied themselves at the barrier, some trying to implant more pickets, others trying to pull them up.[8]

The boundary between church and state does at times seem vague. Since the days when the nation's first president, George Washington, proclaimed a day for public prayer and thanksgiving, U.S. presidents have consistently delivered religious proclamations on Thanksgiving Day. When elected officials are sworn into office or witnesses appear in courts, they take an oath, which to be credible may require placing one's hand on a Bible. In the 1950s the Pledge of Allegiance was revised to insert the phrase "under God" after "one nation." U.S. coins carry the phrase "In God We Trust," which became a national motto in 1955.

No distinct separation between church and state is made when both houses of Congress and state legislatures begin their sessions with prayers offered by chaplains who are paid from tax funds. Although the practice was challenged in 1983, the Supreme Court concluded that legislative prayers were different from mandatory public school prayers. The legislative prayers, the Court ruled, were constitutional because they were not required but instead were part of a traditional practice that had gone on since colonial times.

Separation. In spite of these examples, many of the judges, philosophers, theologians, constitutional lawyers, political scientists, and others who have wrestled for years with church-state issues believe government should not favor one religion over another and should support none.

The Supreme Court has used what is known as a three-part test to determine whether a law violates the

First Amendment. First, to comply with the establishment of religion clause, the law (or government practice) must have a secular purpose. Second, the primary effect cannot be to support or aid religion or to inhibit it. And third, the law or practice must not bring about excessive government involvement with religion.

For decades the Court has required that any disputed law or practice must pass all three tests. But the basis for decisions may be changing. The Court's current chief justice, William Rehnquist, has said that "the 'wall of separation between church and state' is a metaphor based on bad history, a metaphor which has proved useless as a guide to judging. It should be frankly and explicitly abandoned."[9]

Some Court watchers believe that if Rehnquist's view prevails, there will be more government accommodation of religion, particularly in regard to tax aid for parochial schools and government support for various religious activities. Such causes have been aggressively promoted for the past twenty to thirty years by Roman Catholic organizations and some evangelical Protestant groups.

Tax support for religious purposes alarms those who believe that separation of church and state is the foundation for religious freedom. "In a society where there are many religious faiths, no single religious group should benefit from taxes that are paid by people who belong to different denominations or to none," writes history professor Albert Erlebacher of De Paul University, in Chicago.[10] And law professor Norman Redlich at New York University makes the point that proponents of government aid may be depicted as

> *on the side of God and religion, while the opponents are easily characterized as atheistic. . . .*
> *In such a political atmosphere, the rational de-*

fense of constitutional principles becomes increasingly difficult, and religious freedom and diversity are seriously threatened. . . . Church and state are best served by separation rather than by fusion.[11]

3

Free Exercise of Religion

Most Americans who are members of large, mainstream religious groups seldom worry about being able to worship according to their beliefs or being in conflict with accepted customs and laws. But those not part of the mainstream may live by convictions that are contrary to established ways of life or even the social and economic goals of a nation.

In fact, since colonial times, some religious groups in North America have set themselves apart from the larger society. Some separated themselves because they believed in theocracy—rule by God through appointed prophets, priests, or similar officials. Others believed they were guided by direct inspiration from God.

Today, a few separatist groups attempt to live as self-governing communities, or they live within the mainstream of society but try to sustain the religious principles upon which their communities were founded. At times, these principles may collide with local, state, or federal laws. Then people are faced with a choice: to live according to their convictions or to deny their beliefs and comply with the law. In such cases, people may challenge laws that infringe their religious practices. Their cases are usually heard first in state courts or in federal courts (lower than the Supreme Court). They may be appealed to the U.S. Supreme Court, which has the final say on constitutional matters.

What happens when a case reaches the Supreme Court? The Court first decides whether people are objecting to a law for sincere religious reasons and whether that law puts an unfair burden on those who are living by their beliefs.

Until recently, the Court has also used what is called a "compelling interest" guideline. In other words, the religious liberty claim has been denied when there has been a sound and convincing reason for the state or local government to enforce the law (for example, to protect public health). When there has been no overwhelming state interest involved, the Court usually has allowed an exemption for free exercise of a religious practice.

The Pledge of Allegiance. Decisions on the Pledge of Allegiance ceremony provide an example of how adjustments in the law are made. Such religious groups as Jehovah's Witnesses, some Mennonites, and other less well known sects believe that pledging allegiance to any flag is an offense against biblical laws. But until the 1940s, some state laws required schoolchildren to take part in a ceremony pledging allegiance to the flag. Children who did not participate could be expelled from school, and in a few states their parents could be charged with a criminal offense.

In 1940, a member of the Jehovah's Witnesses challenged the mandatory flag salute and pledge, but the Supreme Court upheld the law, saying that the ceremony

Children in a 1940s classroom salute the flag,
as was then required by law in many states.
In 1943, in response to legal challenges by
Jehovah's Witnesses, the Supreme Court ruled
a compulsory flag salute was unconstitutional.

promoted unity and national security. The decision, known as the *Gobitis* case, created great controversy. Some Americans felt the Jehovah's Witnesses were being disloyal and unpatriotic. Frequently, the Witnesses were attacked and their property damaged. At the same time, people who believed that First Amendment rights were being violated by a compulsory flag salute began to protest the Supreme Court decision. Legal experts, religious leaders, and others wrote articles and spoke out in favor of the Witnesses' right to live according to their religious convictions.

Three years later, in *West Virginia State Board of Education* v. *Barnette*, another case involving Jehovah's Witnesses, the Court reversed its earlier ruling, although deciding the case on the grounds that the Witnesses were denied free speech. Justice Robert Jackson noted that local authorities were going beyond their power in compelling a person to "utter what is not in his mind" by saying a pledge. Jackson noted that those who try to eliminate dissent soon begin to destroy the dissenters, a situation that the First Amendment was designed to avoid. "If there is any fixed star in our constitutional constellation, it is that no official . . . can prescribe what shall be orthodox in politics, nationalism, religion, or other matters of opinion or force citizens to confess by word or act their faith therein," Justice Jackson wrote.[12]

Although compelling anyone to recite the pledge was outlawed, many politicians have tried over the years to reinstate a mandatory pledge. In his 1988 presidential campaign, George Bush repeatedly criticized Democratic presidential candidate Michael Dukakis, then governor of Massachusetts, for his stand on a compulsory pledge. Dukakis had vetoed a 1977 state bill that would have required schoolteachers to start each school day by leading their class in reciting the Pledge of Allegiance.

Not only would such a state law have been contested, but the Supreme Court in its 1943 decision had declared such laws unconstitutional. Robert Maddox, executive director of Americans United for Separation of Church and State (or Americans United) noted: "The pledge to the flag speaks of a nation that provides liberty and justice for all . . . [but] to compel any citizen to recite the pledge violates the very freedoms those words guarantee."[13]

Is a Sunday Sabbath Absolute? Some religious groups have clashed with legal codes that require businesses to close on Sundays. Although many Americans observe Sunday as a day of rest in accordance with biblical commandments, the Seventh-Day Adventists are among several religious groups that observe Saturday as the Sabbath. But the Adventists have not always been able to do so freely.

In 1963, for example, Adell Sherbert, a Seventh-Day Adventist living in South Carolina, was working for a textile mill that expanded its work week to six days. She was asked to work on Saturday, but she refused because of her religious beliefs and was fired from her job. Sherbert then applied for unemployment compensation, a program set up in her state as well as others to provide funds for those who lose jobs through no fault of their own.

To qualify for benefits, an unemployed person is usually expected to accept an available job in a similar line of work. But the only mill jobs available to Sherbert also required working six days a week, and she again refused to work on Saturday, the Sabbath that her religion observed. As a result, Sherbert was denied benefits, because the state concluded that she had left her job voluntarily and without good cause. When the case was appealed to the Supreme Court, the justices concluded that the state law had prevented Sherbert from practicing her religion. Thus, the

Court ruled that a state government cannot deny a person unemployment benefits if she or he quits a job that infringes the free exercise of religion.

The Plain People. Another religious group that has had conflicts with state laws is the Amish, who are descendants of Swiss Anabaptists. The Anabaptists were part of the separatist movement in Europe during the Reformation and included groups known as Mennonites, Brethren, and Hutterites. The Anabaptists frequently debated the theology and authority of the Catholic and Protestant churches in Europe. They set themselves apart from everything worldly, believing they should live much as Christians did during the first century.

But divisions occurred within the Anabaptist group, and some members broke away to follow a man named Jakob Ammann (or Jacob Amen), from whom they took their name. Ammann believed in strict religious practices, among them wearing plain clothing and living a simple life based on farming or related occupations like carpentry. The Amish maintained their humble life-style when they emigrated to North America. They would not accept new technology as it developed, such as electricity and modern farm machinery. According to their beliefs, these worldly conveniences would prevent them from being close to nature, where they believe God's presence is felt.

Although the Amish are usually considered the most conservative of the Anabaptist groups, some Mennonites and Brethren also maintain a simple life-style and collectively are known as "plain people." The distinctive clothing worn by the group gives people a sense of belonging, indicates commitment and humility, and helps believers show their separation from the world.[14]

The Amish maintain a more rigid separation from modern society than other Anabaptist groups. They believe that their children should attend school only through

The Amish have rejected many modern conveniences in their determination to remain true to their religious beliefs.

the eighth grade, and they prefer their own church schools to public schools. If adolescents leave the close-knit community to attend a public school all day, the influences of parents and the religious and farming life-style would be weakened, and that, in turn, could eventually destroy Amish communities. Young Amish children learn early that they are needed on the farm and that they make important contributions to their families.[15]

Yet in most states, compulsory education laws require children to remain in school until at least the age of sixteen. In addition, state laws usually require that teachers in parochial schools obtain higher education to qualify for teaching positions. Many teachers in private Amish schools, however, have only an elementary education.

Since Amish schooling violates state laws, how have officials of state governments reacted? During the 1950s and 1960s, several states with large Amish populations began to strictly enforce compulsory education laws, ordering Amish parents to send their children to public schools. But parents refused because of their religious beliefs and were fined and sometimes jailed.

Outside the Amish community these conflicts often became heated, as citizens took sides and law-enforcement officials vowed to do everything in their power to see that the Amish obeyed the laws. Some of the most controversial actions took place in Iowa in 1965. Against the advice of the Iowa attorney general, state truant officers went into an Amish school, planning to force the children to take a school bus to a public school. By forcing school attendance, the officers believed they would make the Amish community comply with school laws, and eventually the problem would be over.

But the press was on the scene when the truant officers arrived. After the story was published, people across the nation criticized the actions of the Iowa school officials. Although the Iowa governor tried to mediate and said he was "more willing to bend laws and logic than human beings," it was not until 1967 that the Iowa legislature changed its school law to allow exemptions because of religious beliefs.[16]

A similar situation existed in Wisconsin during the 1970s. An Amish family refused to obey compulsory education laws, and the case went to the Supreme Court. In this instance, the Court ruled that the compulsory education law would jeopardize the freedom of the Amish to live by their religious beliefs. The Court also ruled that the type of informal vocational (farming) education that Amish children received was in line with the very interests that the state was attempting to protect with its school codes.

Conscientious Objectors. Anabaptist groups such as the Amish, Mennonites, and Brethren, along with other groups like the Quakers, traditionally have been pacifists. That is, they refuse to bear arms even in self-defense and are opposed to war on religious grounds. Other religious groups also have opposed war when it could not be justified in moral terms—"good" attempting to overcome "evil." In fact, many religious groups have taught that believers should refrain from taking part in unjust wars. So when the nation is at war, people who oppose armed conflict on religious, ethical, or moral grounds may face a formidable crisis.

Several times in U.S. history, selective service acts have been passed to require a draft, or compulsory military service, for young men. (Women have been exempt from the draft but have voluntarily joined the armed forces.) Millions of draftees served in World Wars I and II, in the Korean War during the 1950s, and in the war in Vietnam during the 1960s and early 1970s.

In every war, there have been those who have believed strongly that they should not participate in violence or support violent conflicts, and they have refused to fight. Some have applied for conscientious objector (CO) status, which is a legal exemption that allows people to perform noncombat service. COs have worked in hospitals and for the U.S. forestry and highway departments. They also have served as clerks and farmhands.

When American men were drafted to fight in Vietnam, many U.S. citizens opposed the action for religious as well as for a variety of other reasons. As the war went on and more and more U.S. soldiers died in Vietnam, public opposition to the war increased. Thousands of men resisted the draft. Some who were against the war for religious reasons were able to gain CO status. But others resisted by illegally burning their draft cards, or leaving the United States to live in Canada, Sweden, and other countries.

Although public attention focused on a number of well-known people who objected to military service at that time, no CO claim was as widely debated and publicized as that of Muhammad Ali, the former heavyweight boxing champion. Named Cassius Clay at birth, Ali took a new name when in 1965 he became a member and a minister of the Nation of Islam, a controversial black religious group.

In 1968, Ali refused to be inducted into the armed forces, an action which incensed a great number of Americans. Some thought Ali was cowardly; they did not believe he was resisting on religious grounds, even though ministers were automatically exempt from the draft.

The U.S. Department of Justice claimed that Ali simply belonged to a political group. Ali was arrested, convicted of draft evasion, and sentenced to prison. He was also stripped of the title he had won as boxing champion of

At the Houston Army Induction Center, a solemn Muhammad Ali acknowledges his supporters. In a stand that cost him his title as world heavyweight champion, Ali refused military service on religious grounds. His right to do so was later upheld by the Supreme Court.

the world. He spent the next few years appealing his case, which was finally heard by the Supreme Court. In 1971, the Court found Ali's CO status valid and overruled his draft-evasion conviction.

When Ali talked to a sports reporter about his refusal to take up arms, he told his side of the story:

> *In Houston, when I was asked to stand up and be sworn into the service, I thought about . . . all the lynching, raping and killing [black people had] suffered and there was an Army fellow my age acting like god and telling me to go to Viet Nam and fight Asians who'd never called me Nigger, had never lynched me, had never put dogs on me. . . . I said to myself, this guy in the Army suit ain't God—so when he asked me to step forward I just stayed there. . . . I knew the war was wrong, it was against my religious beliefs, and I was willing to go to jail for those beliefs.*[17]

Although the draft was inactivated in 1973, young men today must register after their eighteenth birthday with a selective service board. Registration does not require that a young man serve in the armed forces, but if the draft is initiated once again, eligible men (determined by a lottery and selected from a nationwide computer data bank) would be ordered to serve.

When U.S. troops went to war in January 1991 against Saddam Hussein and his Iraqi forces who had invaded Kuwait, President George Bush and his advisers presented arguments similar to those used during the Vietnam era. They justified armed conflict on the grounds that it was necessary to overcome evil, and most Americans supported the war, according to public opinion polls. But some across the land voiced objections, believing that violence and killing are morally wrong and should be resisted as an act of conscience.

Some young people who had enlisted and were in active duty in the armed forces or were in reserve units applied for discharges as COs. Pacifist organizations and some church groups across the United States received hundreds of calls asking for help in applying for CO status. Officials of the National Interreligious Service Board for Conscientious Objectors, a fifty-year-old organization with headquarters in Washington, D.C., said that two weeks after the Gulf War started they had received more inquiries than in any other war, including Vietnam.[18]

Americans who supported the Gulf War were highly critical of those who applied for CO status while in the armed forces. Since there was no draft, war supporters insisted that men and women who had enlisted should fight. They argued that the objectors had joined the armed forces willingly and just wanted the benefits (such as a paid education) and not the responsibilities that are part of military service.

Those who have counseled COs for years and COs themselves say that some men and women do not face the realities of what war means until after they go through military training. Then they may realize for the first time that they cannot kill or be responsible for leading people under their command to their deaths. But those who file CO claims must show how their beliefs have evolved and explain their religious, moral, or ethical opposition to war. In order to obtain CO status, they must convince military officers that their antiwar convictions are sincere.

Tax Exemptions. For the most part, the guarantee of free exercise of religion has protected people whose beliefs are not shared by the majority of Americans. But the mainstream religious groups also have enjoyed safeguards from some laws—primarily tax codes. State and local governments exempt churches, temples, mosques, and other places of worship and the land on which they are built from the taxes that are applied to other privately owned real estate. The federal government also exempts religious groups, as well as other nonprofit organizations, from income taxes, and individuals may take a tax deduction on their personal income taxes for donations to qualified religious institutions.

According to some scholars, tax exemptions are basic to the free exercise of religion, since they allow a degree of independence. By being exempt from taxes, religious institutions do not support government, and the government stays neutral—does not get entangled with religion. In addition, religious institutions provide some social services, which saves the outlay of tax funds. Thus it is argued that churches deserve special consideration.

However, there also are arguments against tax exemptions for religious organizations. In the first place, the major denominations own billions of dollars worth of property that could be a source of tax revenue. Funds could help support state and local governments, which are expected to provide social services along with regular maintenance of streets, highways, and other public property. The costs of all these services continue to rise, so why shouldn't religious organizations pay their fair share? Critics of religious tax exemptions also ask: Why should those who have no religious affiliation be expected to bear a heavier tax burden to make up for the funds not collected?

Although the tax-exempt status has not been denied often, it can be revoked if many of the activities of a religious organization are devoted to influencing legislation or to campaigning for candidates for public office.

Religious groups, however, are allowed to support political causes, encourage voter registration, and hold nonpartisan programs to hear the views of political candidates.

Federal and state governments also have denied some tax exemptions for religious institutions such as schools and businesses that discriminate against minorities. Religious schools may also be denied a tax exemption if that exemption is held to support a particular religion. In a 1991 case, the Virginia Supreme Court ruled on a lawsuit challenging exemptions provided for Liberty University, which is part of an organization under the leadership of the fundamentalist Protestant minister Jerry Falwell. The state had permitted the school to raise funds by issuing $60 million in tax-free bonds.

Although the school officials insisted Liberty University had toned down its religious emphasis, its admission requirements clearly state that students should comply with evangelistic doctrine. Faculty and staff also are required to be members of Falwell's church and support the church with tithes. The court denied the tax exemption for the university, ruling that the school is a pervasively religious institution and that permitting it to issue tax-free bonds amounted to special treatment or support for one religion, which is unconstitutional.

In recent years, the U.S. Supreme Court and federal circuit courts have heard cases that challenged tax breaks for the sale of religious materials. Except for California, states traditionally did not assess sales tax on Bibles, study manuals, and other religious books and pamphlets that were sold to the public. (No taxes are levied on religious materials that are given away in exchange for donations.) But Jimmy Swaggart, a Louisiana television evangelist, for years had refused to pay the California sales tax on religious materials. His claim was that the tax was unconstitutional.

Lawyers for the Swaggart Ministries argued that the free exercise clause in the U.S. Constitution prohibits the government from taxing print and video materials distributed by religious groups to spread their ideas. But the Court unanimously disagreed. In an opinion written by Justice Sandra Day O'Connor, the justices said that the broad-based California sales tax is "not a tax on the right to disseminate religious information, ideas or beliefs . . ." but a tax on retail sales. The tax law did not single out Swaggart's activities "for special and burdensome treatment," O'Connor wrote. Neither did the state government entangle itself in religious affairs. O'Connor noted there was no attempt to investigate the religious nature of the materials; thus the state was not violating the establishment clause. [19]

A few months after the Swaggart decision, a federal circuit court heard a case brought by a Baptist minister; members of Jewish, Hindu, and Hare Krishna groups; and the North Carolina Civil Liberties Union. The suit challenged a state law that allowed a tax exemption for the sale of Bibles in North Carolina.

Again the decision was unanimous. The justices concluded that exempting Bibles from sales tax while requiring a tax on the sale of other published materials was in effect favoring one religion over another. The exemption "forces the state to discriminate on the basis of the contents of a book, text, or other published work, which is intolerable under the First Amendment," the court said. [20]

4

Restrictions on Religious Practices

Just as tax exemptions for religious groups can be limited, so the right to free exercise of one's religion is subject to some limitations. No right, including the right of free speech and the right of assembly, is absolute.

Sometimes limitations are needed to protect the public welfare. In a highly publicized case in 1989, television evangelist Jim Bakker was convicted of fraud. A jury found that he had used television and other media to solicit funds from viewers who thought they were investing in Christian endeavors. Instead, much of the money was used to support a lavish life-style for Bakker and his wife, Tammy Faye.

In another 1989 case, a federal court in San Jose, California, ruled that a so-called religious school did not have the right to practice medicine. For more than ten years, Arthur Andrews, who called himself a minister, operated the Religious School of Natural Hygiene. He advocated, among other dietary measures, water-only fasts for periods of as long as six weeks to promote good health and overcome disease. At least six people died after following the school's regimen, but because of insufficient evidence the state was unable to charge Andrews in connection with the deaths. The state closed down the school, citing Andrews for operating an unlicensed, illegal medical practice.

Andrews claimed the school was exercising its right to practice its religious beliefs and was exempt from laws governing medical practices. A federal court found otherwise. Andrews was not practicing faith healing, so his religious beliefs did not apply, the court ruled. [21]

Not all restrictions on religious practices can be regarded as measures that protect the general public, however. For example, a rabbi who was an Air Force captain wore a yarmulke (a skullcap) while on duty and was disciplined for the practice. The captain sued the military, claiming that his free exercise of religion had been violated, but the Supreme Court declared that the military was entitled to require a standard dress code for all in the armed forces. To allow variations would threaten discipline and make distinctions between different religious groups, the justices said. (In a dissenting opinion, Justice Sandra Day O'Connor argued that the military had not shown how discipline would suffer if the captain wore his yarmulke.)

Sometimes religious conduct is restricted because it does not conform to community practices. That has been the case with the Hare Krishna religious sect, which frequently solicits funds and sells religious materials in such public places as airports and parks. But during a Minnesota State Fair in 1981, officials limited the sect's activities to certain areas of the fairgrounds. The Hare Krishnas challenged this restriction, but the Supreme Court upheld the right of the state to determine where the Krishnas should conduct their solicitations.

Restraints on Mormon Practices. An early and classic example of how courts place restrictions on religious practices had to do with the Church of Jesus Christ of Latter-day Saints, or the Mormons. The Mormon church was established in the early 1800s under the leadership of Joseph Smith, who called himself a prophet. He declared that he had received revelations from God, which he wrote down in the Book of Mormon. Along with the revelations, considered a supplement to the Protestant Bible, other writings by Smith form the basis for much of the church doctrine.

While many Mormon beliefs are similar to traditional Christian concepts, Smith's claim to have received revelations was offensive if not heretical to most Protestant Americans. In addition, Smith advocated a strict patriarchal rule—men dominated women in family, religious, and civic matters. Mormon men also were expected to practice polygamy (have several wives) whenever possible, a practice that sparked antagonism in areas where Mormons lived.

The Mormons established communities in Illinois, Ohio, and Missouri and gained political power but were forced to leave because of violent mob attacks. One riot killed at least twenty Mormons. When Smith and his brother were shot and killed, the Mormons realized they would have to find refuge far from the Gentiles, as they called non-Mormons.

Brigham Young led the Mormons west to the Great Salt Lake Basin in a territory that later became the state of Utah. Here Young tried to set up a theocracy and continued the unorthodox practice of polygamy. Although the Mormons were hardworking, disciplined people and developed a thriving community in Salt Lake City, many Gentiles hated the sect for their differences.

A political cartoon shows an ax-wielding Uncle Sam attempting to use the anti-polygamy law to attack the Mormon church.

As public antagonism toward Mormonism grew, Congress passed a law in 1862 that banned polygamy. When Mormons continued to live by their church doctrines, dozens of Mormon men in the Utah territory were arrested and jailed for violating a federal law.

One man, George Reynolds, appealed his conviction to the Supreme Court in 1878, but the justices unanimously upheld the lower court's decision. Writing for the Court, Chief Justice Morrison Waite noted that polygamy had always been considered "odious" by people of Western nations. Even though laws could not interfere with religious beliefs, they could restrict unlawful practices, Justice Waite wrote. Since the justices believed polygamy was a social act, not a religious practice, it was subject to legal bans.

In a later case, a Mormon in Idaho challenged a state voting law. At that time (1890), Idaho required voters to swear they did not practice polygamy or belong to any group that advocated multiple marriage partners. Citizens could not cast ballots without taking the oath. The high court upheld the Idaho law with the same arguments used by Justice Waite.

The polygamy issue was finally resolved out of court. Utah applied for statehood, but was not allowed to join the Union until the Mormons agreed to renounce polygamy. After the Idaho case, Mormon leaders announced that polygamy would no longer be sanctioned by the church. Thus, Congress voted to admit Utah as a state.

Some legal experts have questioned whether, during the 1800s, the Mormons were actually allowed to freely practice their religion as guaranteed under the Constitution. The federal government was able to force Mormons to live by mainstream American values. As one scholar put it: "The issue was simple: they could conform or suffer persecution."[22]

Since the early 1900s, the Mormon church has grown and prospered, particularly in the Salt Lake City area. But within the past few years, Mormons have again come under attack from non-Mormons. But the reasons for the conflict are different. Now many non-Mormons believe *their* religious freedom is being denied. Because of the long-held political power of Mormons in Utah, some non-Mormons charge that the church dominates almost every aspect of life in Utah. At least 90 percent of the state legislators and the majority of other state officials are Mormons.

The issue became a matter of public debate in mid-1990, when the American Civil Liberties Union (ACLU) filed a lawsuit on behalf of several students, parents, and teachers against two Utah public school districts. Since the districts allow Mormon prayers to be recited at school functions, the suit charged that public prayers violate the separation of church and state.

Michele Parish-Pixler, executive director of the Utah ACLU, reported that prayer in Utah's public schools is common. Large numbers of Utah's citizens favor the practice, believing that the majority rules, "and if you don't like it, go away." Another attorney pointed out the irony of the situation, noting that Mormons as a minority religious group had suffered religious persecution themselves but may have forgotten their history. [23]

Debates Over Faith Healing. One of the most wrenching of church-state issues is the conflict that arises when the law places limits on people who rely on prayer to heal the sick and injured. A number of rigorous Christian groups are staunchly opposed to medical science and treatment. They believe that only prayer should be used to heal people.

Spiritual healing is also a principal doctrine of the

Christian Science Church, founded by Mary Baker Eddy in the 1870s. Although Christian Scientists are free to choose whatever form of healing treatment they want, most abide by teachings that say sin and disease come about because people are separated from God. Christian Scientists seek to break down barriers between God and themselves through prayer, which, according to the church's doctrine, restores health.

In some instances, Christian Scientists and others who believe in spiritual healing have been forced to accept medical treatment that is against their religious beliefs. The courts are most likely to intervene when the life of a child is threatened. In one case, a Tennessee court ruled that a twelve-year-old girl should undergo drug treatments for cancer in spite of objections from her father, a Pentecostal minister. The father and other members of the family opposed medical treatment on religious grounds.

In another instance, a Massachusetts court ruled that a hospital could use blood transfusions and chemotherapy to treat an eight-year-old suffering from leukemia. The treatments were required even though blood transfusions were prohibited by the religious beliefs of the child's parents, who were Jehovah's Witnesses.

Still another example occurred in Pennsylvania, when a measles epidemic struck dozens of families who were members of two fundamentalist Christian churches. Members of these churches rely on faith healing and refuse medical treatment. Up to seven preschool children died from the disease, and health department officials obtained a court order that allowed doctors to visit homes to monitor seriously ill children. A federal court ordered health officials to force parents to have their children vaccinated against measles.

In spite of such government interventions, many states have passed laws that allow parents to seek spiritual treatment for sick children. The laws are designed to protect parents from charges of neglect if their children are not treated by medical practitioners. But in a number of cases, responsible, caring parents have been convicted of reckless conduct, neglect, or manslaughter when they did not seek medical attention for seriously ill children who died. In these instances, the courts ruled that medical treatment could have been used to prevent the deaths.

Certainly it is a government responsibility to protect the lives of children. But is it a government responsibility to force parents to rely on medical technology? Some people have died under the care of highly competent physicians. Others have been seriously injured or damaged because of some medical practices. So when parents believe that prayer is a lifesaving measure, and through their own experiences have come to the conclusion that prayer heals, are they justified in relying solely on prayer? Are they criminals if they do? And even parents willing to seek medical help in a truly life-threatening situation might not be able to recognize when that occurred.

A majority of Americans, including many legal experts, contend that those who believe in faith healing sacrifice their children for their religious beliefs. But those who sincerely practice spiritual healing believe they are acting according to their conscience and as responsible parents. Some Americans try to find a middle ground by advocating both spiritual and medical treatment to restore health. But the answers do not come easily for some religious people. Instead they pose some of the most difficult issues in regard to the free exercise of religion.[24]

A Far-reaching Curb on Religious Practice. While certainly not a matter of life and death, one recent limitation placed on a religious practice has created an uproar in many parts of the nation and within diverse religious groups. It all began in Oregon, when two Native Americans working for a drug rehabilitation program were fired from their jobs for "misconduct." They had used the drug peyote in religious rituals conducted by Native Americans. Peyote is a nonaddictive drug but is listed as one of the banned substances under Oregon's controlled substance law. However, the federal government and twenty-three other states allow the use of peyote for religious rites, and the federal government allows peyote to be produced and imported.

When the two workers applied for unemployment compensation, they were denied benefits. They filed a suit against the state's employment division, believing their case would be similar to others in which unemployment benefits were denied but reinstated by the court because of religious exemptions. The Oregon Supreme Court did just that, but the case was appealed to the U.S. Supreme Court (*Employment Division* v. *Smith*). Legal experts expected that the Supreme Court would decide the case on the basis of "compelling interest"—the state of Oregon would have to provide convincing reasons that the state law was too important to allow exemptions.

But the Supreme Court did not use the "compelling interest" standard, which had been in effect for nearly thirty years. Instead, in the majority opinion, Justice Antonin Scalia concluded that a person's religious beliefs did not "excuse him from compliance with an otherwise valid law prohibiting conduct that the state is free to regulate." In the past, just the opposite had been true, as, for example, when the Court ruled that the Amish were exempt from compulsory schooling laws.[25]

Justice Scalia also noted in his opinion that religious groups outside the mainstream might lose some liberties, but he declared that this was an "unavoidable consequence" of a democratic form of government. He said that

Outside the Supreme Court, a Native American holy man demonstrates the kind of rituals threatened by laws that may infringe on religious freedom.

the nation could not "afford the luxury" of exempting people from laws that may limit religious practices; although states could pass laws exempting certain religious practices, they were not required to do so. In short, the matter of religious freedom for some groups would depend on whether or not they had enough political power to persuade legislators that their rights needed to be protected.

Justice Sandra Day O'Connor disagreed sharply with Justice Scalia's ruling, saying that it was "incompatible with our nation's fundamental commitment to an individual's religious liberty." In addition, dozens of legal experts, leaders of diverse religious groups, and religious liberty advocates have spoken out against the ruling, calling it a blow to religious freedom and a decision that will have sweeping implications.

How might the ruling be applied? Legal experts say it is possible that minors could be restricted from drinking wine at religious ceremonies (they would not be exempt from state laws banning liquor consumption by minors) and communion wine could be banned in "dry" communities (those that prohibit liquor). People could be punished for violating health laws if they performed rituals such as those required for food preparation in the Muslim and Jewish religions. Laws might prohibit people from wearing certain clothing mandated by their religious doctrines, such as long skirts or head coverings. Instead people would have to comply with dress codes established in workplaces and schools.

Already, court decisions have been revoked. In one case, workers had won religious exemptions to a federal health and safety regulation that required the use of hard hats on construction sites. But in late 1990, the decision was reversed because of the Oregon ruling.

In another instance, a federal judge in Rhode Island had ruled that a family could sue a hospital for performing an unwanted autopsy on their son, who had died from a seizure. According to the family's religious beliefs, it is wrong to mutilate a dead body. But after the Supreme Court decision on the peyote case, the judge had to reverse his decision "with deep regret."[26]

Representative Stephen J. Solarz of Brooklyn, New York, charged that the Court relinquished its role as the guardian of fundamental human rights, leaving these "open to the vagaries of the political process [which] undercuts the very foundations of a constitutional form of government." Solarz, along with fifty-four other members of Congress, introduced a bill called the Religious Freedom Restoration Act of 1990. The act has won wide support in Congress and from religious and other groups that range from conservative to liberal. If passed, the law would overturn the Smith ruling by mandating that courts use the "compelling interest" standard to judge whether a person's free exercise of religion should be denied.[27]

5

Debates Over Religion in Public Schools

Bridget Mergens never intended to make history when, in 1985, she asked her principal's permission to start an after-school Bible club at Westside High School in Omaha, Nebraska. She did not think her idea would pre sent even a slight problem. Mergens assumed her principal would allow a Bible club to "meet like any other club" in the public high school.

Although principal James Findley commended Mergens for wanting to organize a discussion group, he refused to let the club use the school facilities. Why? Because he believed that allowing a Bible club to meet at school would violate federal laws forbidding public schools to endorse a particular religion.

Mergens, on the other hand, thought her free speech rights had been denied. Through a friend, she contacted a legal expert who worked for an organization called the National Legal Foundation (a group founded by television evangelist Pat Robertson, although Robertson no longer has ties with the group). Mergens was advised about the

1984 Equal Access Act, which has been highly controversial. This federal law states that if a public secondary school offers any group activities not related to the curriculum, then that school also must allow equal access to other group functions without discriminating in regard to religious, political, or philosophical beliefs.

The Mergens case traveled through the court system, finally reaching the Supreme Court. In June 1990 the justices ruled in favor of Mergens Mayhew (she had since married). The Court found the Equal Access Act constitutional, basing its decision in part on a 1981 case, *Widmar v. Vincent.* In the Widmar case, the Supreme Court overruled the state of Missouri, which had denied a student group permission to conduct religious discussions and worship services in a University of Missouri building. Although the Court agreed with the state that it should maintain strict separation of church and state, the justices ruled that religious discussions and worship were forms of speech protected by the Constitution.[28]

A number of religious groups hailed the ruling, but some were opposed, believing that equal access means that the public school system can no longer be neutral in regard to religion. Some who have spoken out against the opinion are concerned that schools will have to open their doors not only to many diverse religious groups but also to such groups as satanic clubs and hate groups like the Ku Klux Klan, neo-Nazis, and the Aryan Nation. In addition, there are worries that students will use equal access to proselytize—organize activities to convert their classmates to their religious beliefs.

The Court's ruling on Bible clubs in public schools hardly puts an end to the controversy over religion and education. It represents instead one aspect of a public debate that has led to more lawsuits than any other church-state issue. As one historian noted, "The question of

The Supreme Court's upholding of the 1984 Equal Access Act worries people who fear that the law will be abused.

religion and education is one of the most vexing in the history of American religious liberty."[29]

Early Ties Between Religion and Education. In the early days of America, few people argued about the ties between religion and education. The main purpose of schooling was religious instruction, even after tax-supported grammar schools were established in the mid-1600s. Higher education also was closely linked with religious education. Major Protestant denominations founded or were instrumental in establishing private colleges such as Harvard, Yale, Dartmouth, Rutgers, Columbia, and Brown. Religious groups also were responsible for some of the state universities and maintained their influence over higher education for many years.

Only Virginia, because of the efforts of Thomas Jefferson, established public schools free of church control. Jefferson long had opposed the use of tax funds for religious groups, including church-sponsored schools. After the Revolutionary War, Jefferson pressed for a widespread nonsectarian educational system. He believed a public education system was essential to educate "the common people" and to preserve freedom.

By the early nineteenth century, state legislatures began to pass laws establishing public schools with requirements for public taxation, teacher certification, student attendance, and courses of study. Most state laws prohibited the use of tax funds for religious schools and sectarian instruction in public schools. But the laws allowed general religious teaching, which meant Protestant Christian instruction. In other words, the Protestant Bible was read and Protestant hymns and prayers were used in religious observances. History texts and other books also contained many references to Protestant beliefs.

Yet the nation's citizens were by no means all Protestants. The number of Roman Catholics, for example, grew steadily during the nineteenth century, as an increasing number of immigrants from Catholic countries arrived in America. By mid-century the Roman Catholic Church had become the largest Christian denomination in the United States, and Catholics began to speak out against public schools that were permeated with Protestant teaching, some of it blatantly anti-Catholic. At the same time, the Catholic Church established a parochial school system so that Catholic families could educate their children according to their beliefs.

Maintaining a private school system is expensive, however. As a result, during the 1840s, New York City's Bishop John Hughes began to press for tax funds to support the parochial schools. The bishop argued that Protestant-oriented schools were receiving public monies, so Catholic schools should also be supported by taxes. A bitter political battle followed, with Governor William Seward agreeing with Bishop Hughes. The governor favored an educational system that allowed immigrant children to be taught "by teachers speaking the same language with themselves and professing the same faith." But the New York legislature did not approve tax funds for Catholic schools. Instead, legislators passed a law banning sectarian instruction in public schools while allowing each school district to determine whether a Protestant or a Catholic version of the Bible would be read.[30]

The school issue drove a wedge between Catholics and Protestants. Many Protestants were convinced they were losing "their schools." They also felt threatened by the two million Catholics in the nation, fearing that America would come under the domination of the Roman pope.

By the 1880s and 1890s, the nation included people from an increasing number of diverse religious faiths, including not only Catholics and Protestant denominations

An anti-Catholic mob attacks the state militia in Philadelphia in 1844. Twenty-four people were killed and two Roman Catholic churches burned in a series of riots in the city.

such as Baptists, Presbyterians, Methodists, and Congregationalists, but also such Christian sects as Quakers and Mormons. In addition, many Jews had emigrated from Europe to the United States. The more diverse the population, the more people were bound to challenge Protestant-dominated instruction and exercises in public schools. As a result, most states passed laws requiring public school systems to be neutral on religious matters.

A Continuing Debate. In spite of legislation and court rulings, many public school districts continued to allow Bible readings, school-sponsored prayer, and other religious observances in schools. Still, some parent groups wanted more than religious ceremonies. They thought their children should receive religious instruction as part of their education.

Several types of programs were initiated, allowing students to be released from the regular classroom to attend religious education classes on a voluntary basis. In 1948 these released time programs, as they were called, were declared unconstitutional when they were held in the public schools. Even though attendance in these classes was voluntary, the instruction violated the First Amendment because public schools and religious groups worked together to promote religious teachings. The Supreme Court ruled that a tax-supported institution could not blend religious and secular education and that a compulsory education system could not provide a captive audience for religious instruction. However, later, in the *Zorach* decision of 1952 the Court permitted releasing students to attend religious classes off the public school premises, since the public schools had no further involvement in the program.

During the 1960s, the High Court ruled on several other important cases involving prayer and Bible reading in public schools. In 1962, for example, the New York Board of Regents, the state body governing New York's schools, recommended that each morning students recite a "neutral" prayer that favored no particular religion. But parents of ten students in the New York public schools charged that the practice was unconstitutional. When the case was sent to the U.S. Supreme Court, eight out of nine justices agreed. The Court ruled that state and local governments "should stay out of the business of writing or sanctioning official prayers and leave that purely religious function to the people themselves."

In writing the majority decision, Justice Hugo Black took great care to point out that no hostility to religion should be implied. He wrote that the authors of the U.S. Constitution and Bill of Rights were well aware "that governments of the past had shackled men's tongues to make them speak only the religious thoughts that government wanted them to speak and to pray only to the God that government wanted them to pray to."[31]

The only dissenting justice, Potter Stewart, did not believe that saying a prayer was the same as establishing an official religion. In his opinion, reciting a prayer was simply part of the nation's spiritual heritage—a traditional practice.

Many other Americans also objected to the Court decision, and some members of Congress tried to reverse the decision by drafting constitutional amendments—at least thirty different ones were proposed—to reinstate prayer in the public schools. But there was not enough support to change the U.S. Constitution.

Those who agreed with the ban on school prayer pointed out that no one had been denied the freedom to pray silently no matter where she or he might be. Mandating a specific prayer would impose a religious practice

The Supreme Court's 1962 ruling against school prayer was thought to be the road to ruin by some religious groups.

The Schempp family, shown here on the steps of the Supreme Court, challenged a Pennsylvania law that required ten verses of the Bible to be read in schools each day. In 1963 the Supreme Court ruled the law unconstitutional.

that could be contrary to some students' and their families' beliefs.

In spite of the Court ruling regarding prayer, many public schools continued to recite prayers and read Bible verses, and some states even required prayer and Bible readings. School personnel reasoned that the Court had banned only prayers composed by government officials. But in 1963, the Edward Schempp family in Germantown, Pennsylvania, brought action against their state, which had mandated that ten verses of the Bible be read daily in public school classrooms. As Unitarians, the Schempps found the religious practices in the schools contrary to their beliefs.

The Supreme Court ruled that the Bible-reading requirement was unconstitutional. This ruling, like the one on school prayer, created an uproar among those who contended that the Court decision went against the wishes of the majority in the nation. They argued that the Court was not abiding by the principles of democracy. Yet one of the basic purposes of the Bill of Rights is to prevent the majority—in religious or other realms of society—from oppressing a minority.

Even though President Ronald Reagan and, later, President George Bush called for "voluntary prayer" in the public schools, many religious leaders have emphasized that the Supreme Court has never outlawed *voluntary* prayer. A person can pray privately any time he or she chooses to do so. *Compulsory* prayer and Bible reading, however, could easily become forms of indoctrination, and most major religious groups support bans on mandatory prayer and Bible-reading exercises in public schools.

Nevertheless, a few religious and political groups are pressing for legislation that will require prayer and Bible reading in public schools. In fact, Representative William

Dannemeyer of California proposed a Community Life Amendment to the U.S. Constitution that would allow public school prayers. Many of Dannemeyer's supporters are members of nationally organized fundamentalist and evangelical Christian groups that interpret the Protestant Bible literally. In other words, most believe that everything in their Bible is a strictly factual account, rather than believing that at least some of the stories are allegories or other ways of expressing broad concepts or truths.

Many fundamentalists are associated also with the National Association of Christian Educators and Citizens for Excellence in Education. Directed by Robert Simonds, this organization has hundreds of chapters nationwide and sets up citizen committees to support "Christian candidates" for local school boards.

The citizen committees, as well as fundamentalist organizations, want public schools to reflect what are called "Christian ideals," which could be the same as preaching certain Christian doctrines, a violation of the First Amendment. In addition, the committees want schools to stress "traditional family values." This usually means emphasis on a family structure based on traditional roles for men and women—the father as breadwinner and mother as homemaker and provider of child care. Such a family structure is not found in the majority of U.S. families today, however, and most public schools attempt to show respect for a variety of family forms.

Graduation Prayers. In many communities across the land, public school graduation ceremonies traditionally have begun with prayers. Most of these prayers have been offered by Christian ministers or priests. But not all graduating public school students are Christians. Some may be Unitarians, Jews, Muslims, Hindus, or members of other religious groups. Should a public school graduation cere-

*Members of the Moral Majority
demonstrate outside the Capitol
in Washington, D.C., in 1984, to
show support for a constitutional
amendment that would permit
prayer in public schools.*

mony then begin with prayer that some graduates would find offensive or feel uncomfortable about?

To respond to that question, some schools have asked clerics to recite nondenominational prayers. But some legal experts argue that prayer—no matter how neutral it might be—in a public school is, because of that setting, a government-sponsored prayer and unconstitutional. Others argue that graduation prayers should be allowed because they are traditional and inspiring to the graduates. The issue has divided communities in a number of states and resulted in state and federal court cases. But rulings have not been clear-cut.

In 1991, the Supreme Court agreed to hear a case called *Lee* v. *Weisman*, which had begun three years earlier in Providence, Rhode Island. At that time, the Daniel Weisman family had won a federal court suit in which they had objected to graduation prayers. The court ruled the practice unconstitutional. But Providence school officials appealed, and the U.S. Justice Department, with the backing of President George Bush, urged the High Court to hear the case.

Targeting Textbooks. Along with requiring prayer in public schools, some religious groups also want the curriculum and the textbooks to reflect Christian doctrine. Parent groups in a number of states have tried to ban the use of reading texts that include classic stories such as *The Wizard of Oz*, *Cinderella*, and the tales of King Arthur. Why do parents want to keep this literature out of the classroom? Because fundamentalists contend that the stories promote belief in magic and the occult. Even a popular version of the story of the *Three Little Pigs* has been attacked. Some parents claim the story promotes witchcraft, because the three pigs dance around the wolf in a boiling kettle.

The Diary of Anne Frank, which describes the beliefs of Judaism, and other texts that include descriptions of Hinduism and other religious beliefs have been attacked because they do not jibe with fundamentalist doctrines. Some fundamentalists also claim that public schools are promoting "secular humanism." This term, used almost as a curse, usually refers to a philosophy or moral view that does not support Christian doctrine. One simplified example would be teaching a young person to develop self-esteem and self-reliance. That teaching could be construed by some Christian groups as being "godless," because the young person is not encouraged to seek help from a supreme being. But the fact that public schools do not teach a religious doctrine does not mean that public schools teach a "godless philosophy," which some have labeled secular humanism.

In spite of the many charges against secular humanism, the philosophy is not taught in the public schools. In fact, very few public school teachers would be able to define what secular humanism is. Even among the diverse humanist groups in the United States, few would agree on how secular humanism, civil humanism, or just plain humanism should be defined. Some humanist groups consider themselves secular; others call themselves religious. Basically, though, most humanists of all factions believe in moral values based on regard for humanity, values that probably have their roots in ancient Greek philosophy. Many humanists also believe they share values common to a variety of religious groups. "Humanist views of moral and social issues are shared widely by Christian, Jewish, and other Americans," says Edd Doerr, executive director of Americans for Religious Liberty, who writes frequently for *The Humanist* magazine and other publications.[32]

However, some religious groups continue to condemn public school curricula and textbooks for their alleged

Activists such as Mel Gabler of Texas have tried to block textbooks that do not reflect what they consider to be correct values.

humanist leanings. For years, a group of religious funda-mentalists in Texas has been "reviewing" nearly all curric-ulum materials that are considered for use in that state's public schools. Initiated in 1961 by Mel and Norma Gab-ler, these self-appointed reviewers try to block the pur-chase of science texts that teach evolution, family living texts that include sex education or show women in non-traditional roles, or American history texts that describe events such as slavery, the Vietnam War, and Watergate in an unfavorable way. The Gablers have declared that the textbooks they oppose give students ideas and set the stage for students to question the values they have been taught at home.

The Gablers and their activities have generated a great deal of publicity, because Texas is one of the largest buyers of textbooks in the country. Thus publishers may gear their materials to fit what the Texas Board of Educa-tion decides is appropriate. Yet after years of prohibiting the teaching of evolution, Texas recently developed guide-lines that require biology texts to include a section on evolution. In addition, the board has rejected attempts to delete classic literature from reading textbooks.

Creationism Controversy. Texas is not the only state where there has been controversy over the scientific theory of evolution. In some states, schools have required the teaching of creationism along with evolution, or have re-quired that all references to the theory of evolution be dropped from biology text materials. Creationism is a belief that the world and humankind were created literally as described in the biblical book of Genesis. Basically, the evolution theory, which Charles Darwin and others devel-oped by scientific methods, explains how plants, animals, and humans gradually evolved through a natural process.

The debates over creationism and evolution are not new. Many people are familiar with the story of John T. Scopes, a young biology teacher in Tennessee during the 1920s. Scopes taught his class Darwin's theory of evolution. At that time, Tennessee law banned any teaching that denied "the story of the divine creation of man as taught in the Bible," and Scopes was sued for violating the law. Scopes was convicted, and Clarence Darrow, Scopes's lawyer and a famous defense attorney, threatened to take the case to the U.S. Supreme Court. But the Tennessee Supreme Court eventually reversed the decision of the trial court.

About the time of the Scopes trial, Arkansas too had enacted a law prohibiting the teaching of evolution. Some forty years later, Susan Epperson, an Alabama high school teacher, challenged the law. This time, the case reached the High Court, and in 1968 the Court ruled that the Arkansas law was unconstitutional. It violated both the First and Fourteenth Amendments. The Court declared that Arkansas had tried to prevent its teachers from discussing the evolution theory because it was contrary to the beliefs of some that the book of Genesis was the only authority on human origin.

The Court decision did not end efforts to promote creationism. Believers have pressured schools to teach creationism as a "science"—an "alternative theory" to evolution. Since the Epperson decision, legislators in about two dozen states have tried to pass laws that would mandate the teaching of "scientific creationism." But major church denominations and civil liberties groups have opposed such efforts, pointing out that creationism is not a science, and teaching it would be promoting a religious belief, which is prohibited in the public schools.

Even if a large majority of the citizens in a commu-

*John Scopes, flanked here by lawyers
Dudley Malone (left) and Clarence Darrow
(right), was tried for teaching his students
Darwin's theory of evolution.*

nity believe that creationism should be taught, the courts have ruled that the public school is not the place to advance sectarian ideology, or a particular religious view. Public schools must remain neutral and teach a range of ideas. But Americans do have the freedom to teach religious beliefs in their homes and at religious institutions, such as churches, temples, and parochial schools.

Teaching About Religion. Although public schools are required to be neutral in regard to religious views, they can teach *about* religion. Yet the role of religion in world history and in many current events frequently is ignored, perhaps because school administrators fear controversy. In some cases, teaching about religion would mean including stories of brutal repressions and "holy wars" that do not reflect favorably on religion.

A number of educators and citizen groups, however, believe that to understand history adequately, people need to learn how religion relates to the development of civilization. "A person totally ignorant of religion is only partially educated," wrote Richard P. McBrien, theologian and syndicated columnist.[33]

How can public schools teach about religion, but at the same time refrain from indoctrinating students in a particular belief? To answer that question, fourteen national organizations have cooperated in the preparation of guidelines for distribution to public schools. The sponsoring organizations include the American Academy of Religion, American Association of School Administrators, Americans United Research Foundation, National Conference of Christians and Jews, National Council on Religion and Public Education, National Education Association, and National School Boards Association. They advise public schools to approach religion as an academic subject, not as a devotional practice. The group also advises that students be educated about all religions but not pressured to accept any one religious view, and that the role of religion in history and society be presented without promoting or belittling any belief.

Finally, the group points out that the study of religion is important "if students are to value religious liberty, the first freedom guaranteed in the Bill of Rights. Moreover, knowledge of the roles of religion in the past and present promotes cross-cultural understanding essential to democracy and world peace."[34]

Tax Funds for Private Schools? Another church-state controversy in regard to public education has become heated in recent years. The question: Should public tax money be used to help finance private schools, a large majority of which are parochial schools? So far, in states where tax funds for parochial schools have been challenged, the Supreme Court has struck down such practices. The Court has barred parochiaid, as it is called, to pay teacher salaries, buy teaching materials, or pay building maintenance expenses. Yet for several decades some religious and political organizations have been able to convince state governments to funnel tax money to parochial schools through a variety of programs.

In Louisiana, parochiaid has been provided for more than two decades. A federal district court in 1990 ruled that part of Louisiana's parochiaid program was unconstitutional because it supported a specific religion and involved excessive entanglement of church and state. Catholic parents, backed by the U.S. Catholic Conference and the U.S. Justice Department, are attempting to retain the aid. But a local taxpayer group and national educational organizations oppose channeling tax funds or services and equipment paid for with public funds to Catholic parochial schools.

*Students at a Roman Catholic parochial
school participate in religious services
during their school day.*

In other parts of the nation, some parent groups want legislation passed that would allow them to deduct a percentage of the amount they spend for their children's private school tuition from their federal or state income taxes. Others advocate a federal or state aid program allowing parents to use a voucher that guarantees government payment of tuition for any children who transfer from public to private schools.

A voucher system has been touted recently by nonsectarian groups, as well as by religious groups such as Catholics, Lutherans, and others that operate parochial schools. Those who favor what have been dubbed "choice" plans for education also endorse using public vouchers to subsidize choices in the schools children attend. Proponents say that parents should be able to send their children to schools that teach according to parents' beliefs. Another major argument for choice is that public schools would improve if they were faced with private school competition, as businesses are faced with competition in the marketplace.

Opponents of choice plans point out that public schools are not able to operate in a free-market economy like service businesses. They are subject to laws that forbid discrimination on the basis of race, gender, income, language, handicaps, and other factors. Unlike private schools, public schools cannot accept only those students they wish to serve.

Critics of choice plans also contend that tax funds would be diverted from public schools, many of which are struggling with money problems already. Some public schools might be forced to close because of lack of funds, perhaps leaving parents with only the option of a private school education for their children or transporting their children long distances to another public school.

If voucher systems or other schemes to provide public funds for private schools were adopted on a widespread basis, private schools accepting public funds would be subject to government regulations. This could result in unwanted government intervention or restrictions on the exercise of religion. U.S. Education Secretary Lamar Alexander has stated that regulations would be needed to make certain that no tax funds went to "weird" schools. But legal difficulties could arise in determining which schools are suspect and which are not. Some religious schools might appear "weird" if they taught doctrines not shared by the mainstream or by the officials who set the rules for tax aid eligibility.

Those who advocate church-state separation believe public funds should be restricted to schools where no religious doctrine is taught and students of all religious persuasions or with no religious affiliations are welcome. Separationists want to exercise the right to donate *only* to religious groups of their choice. They agree with Jefferson, who said long ago that it is "sinful and tyrannical" to compel people to contribute funds to aid in imparting views in which they do not believe.[35]

*Religion
and
Politics*

As public debate over the ties between government and public education continues, the arguments sometimes go well beyond the legal and constitutional questions. They focus instead on the much broader issue of how religious beliefs should or should not affect American political life.

Most of us are aware of the concept that the government (local, state, or federal) cannot establish a state church, and no church can speak for the government. But the majority of Americans may not be aware of the close ties between religion and politics in the United States.

Certainly, the main function of religious organizations is meeting the spiritual needs of members. But from America's earliest days, religious leaders and groups have taken stands on many political issues. Author Garry Wills, who has written extensively on religion in American life, notes that religion plays a much larger role in U.S. elections and government policies than most people think. Religious beliefs frequently influence how people vote and the kind of pressure they bring on politicians to enact legislation to fit their particular views.[36]

Religious Forces Worldwide. Religious forces have been behind many political movements, not only in the United States but throughout the world as well. India's Hindu leader Mohandas K. Gandhi, who led a nonviolent campaign from the 1920s through the 1940s to free India from British rule, once said: "If you believe that religion has nothing to do with politics, then you don't understand religion."[37]

In some countries in the Middle East, Islamic, or Muslim, religious leaders have had great influence on or controlled governmental affairs. The Ayatollah (a religious title meaning "sign of God") Ruhollah Khomeini established an Islamic republic in Iran in 1979. Islam is often called a religion of laws, as taught by the prophet Mohammed. When Khomeini took power, he ordered his followers to "comply or be obliterated." Until his death more than a decade later, Khomeini's repressive regime tortured and executed countless opponents, particularly among non-Muslim groups such as the Baha'is. More than one hundred Baha'i leaders were executed, and thousands of Baha'is left the country. The nation still lives by Islamic laws, including the requirements that students study Islam and that women wear veils.[38]

Although some nations are controlled by religious doctrine and laws, religious views more often influence government than act as a basis for authority. In other words, religious doctrine does not necessarily determine laws. For example, until about the mid-1900s, the Catholic Church in such European nations as France, Italy, and the Netherlands directed parishioners to support certain political parties with their votes. But that did not mean the Catholic Church took over the government, because people had the freedom to vote as they pleased.

The church still has significant political impact, particularly in Latin American countries and in Ireland and

Iranian women hold a poster depicting Ayatollah Khomeini. Following the Islamic laws introduced by the Ayatollah, they wear the chador, *a veil that covers the body from head to foot.*

Poland. The Roman Catholic Church of Poland was a leading force in the ouster of Communism. The church has been able to make extensive demands regarding the nation's social policies, and church leaders have pressured for laws that restrict abortion, certain forms of sex education, and divorce.[39]

In Britain, some leaders of the Church of England are automatically members of the House of Lords—the upper house of Parliament—and, as described previously, the Anglican Church had great political power in colonial America. Protestant groups also were able to shape political agendas during the colonial period and early days of statehood in the United States.

Few religious groups developed political goals based on such ideals as harmony and equality for all people, however. For centuries, many Christian groups believed that Africans brought to America as slaves and Native Americans were "subhuman" and fit for little except serving "superior whites." On this basis, landowners justified enslaving blacks and in the Southern states used slave labor to develop plantations.

Most churches in the South condoned slavery, supporting the practice with the biblical story of the curse placed on Ham, the son of Noah, in the book of Genesis. (It was claimed that black people were descended from Ham, and shared the curse.) Yet some religious groups in the North (but by no means all) made the abolition of slavery a moral crusade. Many in the abolitionist movement believed that slavery was contrary to biblical teachings. Thus, in the Civil War, both those for and those against slavery declared the war had been sanctified by God. And people on each side believed they were taking part in a holy and just war to exterminate the evil of the other.

Bigotry and Discrimination. Before and after the Civil War, some white Protestants of English and other northern European ancestry also were prompted by a sense of religious "superiority" to justify acts of bigotry and discrimination against Catholics. From about 1830 to the 1850s, some Protestant church leaders and politicians known as Nativists (because they were native-born Americans) conducted bigoted, savage campaigns against Catholics. At the turn of the century, similar tactics were used by people who wanted to restrict the number of immigrants coming into the United States from nations in southern and eastern Europe, primarily Catholic countries.

From the beginning of the 1900s to about mid-century, Christian groups—both Catholic and Protestant—turned against Jews. Widespread anti-Semitism was partially due to a fear that Jews were agents for Russian communists who, it was believed, were attempting to take over the world. In addition, false documents were published in the United States to imply that Jewish leaders were attempting to control banks and world trade.

Eventually the Federal (now National) Council of Churches and some prominent Americans denounced the propaganda. But blatant anti-Semitism prevailed for many years. Charles E. Coughlin, a Catholic priest in Michigan, helped fuel the anti-Semitic rhetoric with radio broadcasts in which he repeatedly implied that a Jewish conspiracy would take over the world economically. Although the church ordered him to stop preaching his bigoted ideas, Coughlin's message was taken up by some Protestant preachers and by American Nazis and other semimilitary groups.

Over the years, other groups claiming religious ties have tried to establish ways of life based on discriminatory practices, hate, and violence. The Ku Klux Klan (KKK),

Anti-Semitic and racist messages find ready audiences among people who fear those different from themselves. The Rev. Charles E. Coughlin, although not supported by the Roman Catholic Church, used his position as a priest to promote his views.

for example, has been in existence since the 1860s, although its membership has waxed and waned. The Klan maintains that it is Christian and patriotic. But KKK members have consistently shown disdain for Christian beliefs and democratic principles, both of which respect the dignity and worth of people from diverse backgrounds and heritage. Many members of the Klan have been consumed with hate for people different from themselves and have physically attacked, tortured, and killed fellow Americans, sometimes with the silent support of law officials and community leaders.

The Civil Rights Movement. During the late 1950s and 1960s, however, religion and politics linked to try to combat bigotry, racism, and discriminatory practices against people of color and non-Christians. At that time, members of minority groups were barred from some communities and jobs and also were excluded from many schools, private clubs, hotels, and other facilities. In southern states, segregation of blacks and whites was a way of life, and voting rights were denied to blacks in most communities.

African-American protests against discrimination, and the struggle for voting and other civil rights, began with black ministers and their congregations and with the legal activities of such groups as the National Association for the Advancement of Colored People (NAACP) and the Urban League. Martin Luther King, Jr., the well-known civil rights leader and Baptist minister, had long believed it was a moral duty to work for social justice. Although he stressed the importance of obeying laws, he advocated civil disobedience, or breaking laws that were unjust, such as those that prevented people of color from voting. He was willing to go to jail for his civil disobedience.

Many Americans believe the civil rights movement was primarily political in nature. But it was based on

The Ku Klux Klan, which claims to be a Christian group, has terrorized those it considers a threat.

concepts common to Judaism and Christianity, and shaped by ministers such as King, who "perceived his leadership as fundamentally religious," as one scholar explained. King's "style of speaking, the cadence of his voice, the choice of words and images, all echoed his church background and evoked, no less than the substance of his message, the rich tradition of black religion. In King, social justice and religion seemed inseparable."[40]

Through the 1960s and 1970s, many religious groups, including Jews, mainstream Protestants, and Catholics, joined the civil rights movement. Some pressured political leaders to pass civil rights laws that would help bring about social and economic justice for people of minority groups. The Civil Rights Act of 1964 made it illegal to discriminate in employment and housing on the basis of racial and ethnic background, and the Voting Rights Act of 1965 banned discriminatory practices in voting.

Some religious groups helped support school desegregation and to oppose gender bias in employment. In the late 1960s, the Supreme Court issued a number of rulings requiring school boards to develop and implement plans for school desegregation, mandated by landmark 1954 federal legislation. In addition, laws and court cases attempted to ban discrimination against women in jobs, education, politics, and other aspects of society. Through political channels, religious leaders also sought to overcome social ills like poverty and homelessness.

Current Debates Over Religion and Politics. Although diverse religious groups have formed coalitions to work toward the common good, they also have been divided on many controversial questions, splitting into conservative and liberal camps. In general, conservative Protestants press for a moral code that is based on literal interpretations of biblical precepts. Conservative evangelicals also stress Bible study and a "born-again gospel," or accepting Jesus Christ as a personal savior. Liberal religious groups, on the other hand, are more likely to stress social concerns. They usually respect diverse religious beliefs, recognizing common threads among varied theological views.

In the political arena, some conservative religious groups are demanding that the nation's people live by Christian values, and that these values should dominate our government. Yet many Americans live by moral or ethical values that may not be tied to a Christian or any other religious doctrine. In the view of many citizens, public policies should reflect the diversity of religious and nonreligious views in the United States and recognize that morality is not always shaped by religion.

Heated debates also arise over such moral issues as whether sex education should be given in public schools, what should be labeled pornographic, the rights of homosexuals, whether terminally ill people should be allowed to die or be assisted in dying if they so choose, and whether the nation should become involved in war. One of the most controversial and emotionally charged issues, however, is abortion. It often creates hostile divisions between people.

On one side are conservative groups such as fundamentalist and evangelical Protestants who have aligned themselves with Catholics to oppose abortion. Most of these groups are pressuring for laws that will end a woman's right to choose for herself whether she will terminate an unwanted or unsafe pregnancy. The National Conference of Catholic Bishops stated in 1989 that no Catholic should take a pro-choice position (that is, favor abortion). Frequently, these and other religious leaders, including many TV evangelists, have denounced political candidates who do.

The issue of a woman's right to terminate a pregnancy continues to spark debate between pro-choice and anti-abortion groups.

Bishop Austin B. Vaughan, for example, declared publicly that New York Governor Mario Cuomo could go to hell because of his views on abortion. Cuomo had stated that regardless of his own opposition to abortion he would not impose his beliefs on others and was duty-bound to allow women to exercise their reproductive rights. Leo T. Maher, a Catholic bishop in San Diego, California, banned one of his parishioners, Lucy Killea, a pro-choice candidate for the state assembly, from taking communion. Killea declared that she had the right to her own beliefs about a woman's choice in regard to abortion. She subsequently won election to office, defeating an anti-choice candidate.

Religious coalitions have also formed to keep abortion legal and to protect the reproductive rights of women. These coalitions include Episcopalians, Presbyterians, members of the United Church of Christ, Unitarians, and some Jewish groups. They believe that decisions regarding abortion should be made according to the conscience of individuals involved, not by the state.

Several years ago, thirty-six religious organizations sought a Supreme Court decision that would prevent Missouri state laws from restricting abortion. Lawyers representing the group explained in their court brief:

> *Judicial protection of the privacy of pregnant women is not a decision to favor or even approve abortion, but instead a commitment to preserve individual autonomy. That, of course, must be the lodestar in a country as diverse and as committed to freedom as ours. The Supreme Court's role in preserving the space for the free exercise of personal and religious conscience is never more crucial than where there is massive public turmoil surrounding the subject. Otherwise, ma-*

jorities, and even mobilized minorities, can invoke the power of the state to curb the religious freedoms of those they do not like.[41]

Religious Symbols on Public Property. Until recent years, the varied religious beliefs of Americans usually have been ignored when it comes to placing religious symbols and displays on public property. In cases brought before state and federal courts across the United States, from Connecticut to California and Michigan to Florida, judges have ruled that religious symbols such as crosses should not remain on public buildings or be used on public documents. In Arizona, for example, a Superior Court judge ruled in 1990 that a cross atop a chapel on the Arizona State University campus had to be removed because the cross violated the constitutional provision for separating church and state.

A year later, in Illinois, a federal appeals court determined that two communities, Rolling Meadows and Zion, could not use municipal seals—emblems placed on city stationery, police cars, and other property—with religious symbols. The emblems of both communities included a cross, which does not represent a particular Christian denomination but certainly is a symbol for Christianity.

The Rolling Meadows seal was designed to depict various segments of the community and, along with a cross on a church, included a school, water tower, and factory. The Zion emblem depicted a crown and scepter and a banner reading "God Reigns." While the Rolling Meadows seal was created as an art project with no religious intent, the Zion seal had been used for nearly one hundred years to reflect the city's original purpose—it was founded as a theocracy.

The appeals court recognized the historic nature of the Zion symbol but ruled that "the city may not honor its

In Zion, a city in Illinois founded on religious principles, religious doctrine once permeated every aspect of people's lives. In 1991 a federal appeals court ordered the city to remove the religious images on its municipal seal.

history by retaining the blatantly sectarian seal, emblem and logo. These symbols transcend mere commemoration, and effectively endorse or promote the Christian faith." In the court's opinion, the seals for both Zion and Rolling Meadows contained "sectarian religious imagery [that] simply has no place on municipal seals."[42]

Other debates over symbols have centered on holiday displays, particularly those used at Christmas. As is well known, Christmas is a holiday with religious roots—a celebration of the birth of Christ. Although many Americans suggest that the spirit of Christmas giving and good will can be celebrated by all regardless of their religious beliefs, the fact remains that Christmas is distinctly Christian. It is a legal holiday, but it is not, as some would suggest, simply a secular event.

Yet millions of Americans—Jews, Muslims, members of Eastern religious groups, and even some Christians—do not celebrate Christmas. Some reject it altogether, since the very act of celebrating Christmas would be against their beliefs. The fact that Christmas is considered a national holiday suggests that the United States is a Christian nation that excludes American citizens who are not part of the Christian mainstream.

For more than a century some American Jews have compensated for this exclusion by emphasizing Chanukah, the festival of lights. Historically, Chanukah was never a major Jewish observance, according to Judaism scholar Jonathan D. Sarna. He points out that the festival has "succeeded somewhat in placating Jewish children who longed for the gifts and pageantry that their Christmas-observing Christian friends enjoyed." But the "Christmas problem" for Jews and members of other religious groups has never been resolved, and it is one of the reasons that tension arises when Christmas displays appear on public property.[43]

In many communities across the United States, angry controversy has erupted when some citizens have objected to a crèche, or Nativity scene, on the lawn of a municipal building or in a public park, square, or other government-owned area. These citizens see displaying a Nativity scene on public property as government support for a particular religion. However, some Christians believe that such Nativity scenes are just part of the national holiday observance, and that the concepts of majority rule and free exercise of religion should be applied when determining whether the crèche is displayed. They have suggested that non-Christian religious groups also display symbols, such as the Jewish menorah, or candelabrum, in public places.

The debate over public display of holiday symbols has prompted lawsuits, and two reached the Supreme Court in recent years, resulting in rulings that seem contradictory but are not. In a 1989 Pittsburgh case, the Court ruled that a menorah may be displayed along with secular symbols on government property. The reason is that the menorah is not necessarily a symbol of a religious observance. It symbolizes the festival of lights and marks a victory over forces trying to destroy Judaism. The menorah in question was erected on city property along with a sign that read "Salute to Liberty," which linked it to a secular event.

The High Court also ruled in 1989 that a Nativity display is specifically religious if it stands alone on public property and is not displayed with secular symbols like Santa Claus and his reindeer. A Nativity display without secular decorations appears to be an endorsement of a particular religion, and thus is unconstitutional.

There is no question about the legality of religious displays on private property. In some communities, government officials avoid arguments when they require that religious displays appear *only* on private property, such as a home or church lawn.

Should Political Leaders Proselytize? Whatever the controversies over religious issues, the majority of Americans apparently believe that organized religious groups should be involved in public policy debates. An Associated Press telephone poll in late 1990 found that at least 75 percent of the 1,006 Protestants and Catholics surveyed said it was acceptable for religious leaders to speak out on public policies, although only about 34 percent believed religious leaders should endorse political candidates.[44]

But what about politicians who are elected to office and public officials who are appointed? Should they publicly express their religious views? Should government officials make decisions based on their religious beliefs if those beliefs are contrary to the religious views of some of their constituents? There are no clear-cut answers to these questions, and they have sparked as much controversy as religious opinions themselves.

In some cases, the religious beliefs of one group have prompted public officials to try to deny the rights of some other groups. Representative William Dannemeyer of California, for example, has argued that homosexuals have no civil rights. He and his supporters believe that homosexuality is sinful, and he has urged Christians to fight the increasing political power of homosexual groups.

Sheriff Jim Hickey in Nueces County, Texas, created conflict in 1990 when he declared that, because of his religious beliefs opposing abortion, he would not arrest antiabortionists who blocked the doorway of an abortion clinic. The protestors were illegally trespassing on private property, and as a public official Hickey was required to enforce the law. But he said that his first duty was to God.

The views of the congressman and the sheriff raise another question: Can public officials who hold deep religious beliefs follow their conscience and still support a democratic form of government?

Many have done just that. They have been able to maintain their personal faith but not impose it on others. In the 1960s, John F. Kennedy, the first Roman Catholic to be elected president, stated on a number of occasions that church and state should be separate and that no religious leader should dictate how a president should act or how citizens should vote. President Jimmy Carter publicly declared his religious beliefs and his principles of service to and sacrifice for others. But Carter was committed to maintaining the separation of church and state while at the same time exercising his right to live by his deeply held religious beliefs. He also had a great respect for others' religious views, and according to one author was "scrupulously impartial in dealing with all organized churches and religious bodies."[45]

Although some public officials have made clear their positions on moral issues, many have been vague about their religious, moral, or ethical beliefs. Nevertheless, the majority of Americans expect public officials themselves to live and act according to moral principles—to be honest, have integrity, and exhibit respect for people and property. But most citizens object to a government that tries to coerce or even tries to persuade citizens to act contrary to their own beliefs.

Whose Way of Life Is "Right?"

- In Connecticut, Planned Parenthood threatened a lawsuit—on church-state grounds—against a local school board. Members had canceled a public school health fair because the agency was participating. A parent group thought that students should not be exposed to the agency because of its pro-choice view on abortion. But because of the possible lawsuit, the board agreed to hold the health fair and to allow Planned Parenthood to be part of it.

- In California, Stephen Last, an atheist, tried to protest the practice of offering a prayer before a county government meeting. As a citizen, Last believed that he should be able to attend and participate in a public meeting, but that government should not force religious practices upon him. County officials said they would continue opening their sessions with prayer, arguing that they had just as much right to do so as does the U.S. Congress. Last, meantime, was charged with a misdemeanor for disturbing a public meeting.

■ In Indiana, an employer threatened to fire a Muslim man because of the man's opposition to the 1991 war in the Persian Gulf. The employer supported the U.S. military offensive against Iraq, while the Muslim worker questioned the morality of armed conflict and the stereotypical belief of many Americans that Muslims thrive on killing or are a violent people—concepts that are false. Although the Muslim man was not fired, the Islamic Society was prepared to take legal action had such action occurred.

■ In Missouri, a group of parents and students challenged a ban on public school dances in the small town of Purdy. Most of Purdy's residents, who are fundamentalists and believe dancing is sinful, supported the ban. Although a district court ruled that the ban was unconstitutional, a higher circuit court overturned the decision, declaring the ban was "neutral" since all citizens were allowed to take part in determining public policies. The U.S. Supreme Court allowed the decision to stand without comment.

These, along with other examples that have been described throughout this book, represent the conflicts and difficulties posed when deciding whose moral values are "right." Sometimes public officials or others in authority appear to determine moral codes for all people. Other times, a religious group seems to impose its beliefs on government and in turn on the people who are governed. Either way there is tension.

Us vs. Them. When one group decides its religious views are "right" and others are "wrong," the stage is set for conflict. Consider the religious squabbles in the city of Zion, Illinois, just north of Chicago.

Zion was founded in 1900 as a "holy city" by John Alexander Dowie, a minister from Scotland who called himself a prophet and "divine healer." He claimed to have healed hundreds of individuals through prayer, although his healing practices violated civil laws and he was arrested hundreds of times.

Dowie was able to organize an independent Protestant church called the Christian Catholic Apostolic Church, which drew thousands of members from across the United States. He also managed to establish a community based on a doctrine of faith healing, communal living, and strict adherence to biblical laws such as the Old Testament bans on eating pork and shellfish. Only members of the church were allowed to live in Zion City. According to Dowie, the land was "divinely owned," so residents were allowed to build homes but only lease the land from the church organization.

In order to provide income for the faithful, the church developed industries, stores, a printing and publishing company, and other businesses. Church members built a four-story religious school and a 350-room Divine Healing Home, where visitors could live while waiting for their healings.

Although Zion City grew rapidly to a population of about 20,000 and prospered for a time, the church ran into financial difficulties after Dowie's death. A new leader, Wilbur Glenn Voliva, began an extensive publicity campaign to urge those who believed in the church to "sell your outside properties and come with all your house [that is, your household] and your money to help build the city." But in order to stay solvent, the church had to sell some of its land and buildings to "outsiders," and the town began to change, although not without conflict.

There were many court battles over city laws that newcomers and visitors thought were unconstitutional. Because of the church doctrine of faith healing, city ordinances had been passed outlawing vaccinations even dur-

This drawing from the early 1900s depicts the spirit of "Christian cooperation" that was supposed to govern Zion, Illinois.

ing smallpox epidemics. A law also prohibited smoking in any public place. Such laws are now common, but Zion's antismoking law was rigidly enforced, sometimes at the expense of people's privacy. Police officers and church officials stopped cars and boarded trains passing through town and arrested the smokers, or "stinkpots," as they were contemptuously labeled.

City officials also confiscated truckloads of food products if any contained forbidden foods or alcoholic beverages. On one occasion, officers stopped a truck carrying a load of canned pork and beans, destroying the load before allowing the driver to go on.

As more and more "outsiders" moved into the community, the church faithful felt increasingly threatened. Church leaders put up huge billboards along the city's main street. One was a "Perfectly Plain Notice" in bold capital letters asserting:

THIS CITY WAS ESTABLISHED BY THE CHRISTIAN CATHOLIC CHURCH . . . AND THE PRIVATE HOME OF ITS OFFICERS AND MEMBERS. NO GENTLEMAN NOT TO MENTION A CHRISTIAN WOULD BREAK INTO A CHURCH SETTLEMENT AND ATTEMPT TO . . . ESTABLISH A COUNTER ORGANIZATION. THOSE WHO DO ARE NOTHING MORE NOR LESS THAN RELIGIOUS BUMS, TRAMPS AND VAGABONDS WITH LESS HONOR THAN A GANG OF HIGHWAY ROBBERS AND THUGS. GET OUT OF THIS COMMUNITY IF YOU HAVE A DROP OF HONEST BLOOD AND GO ESTABLISH A SETTLEMENT OF YOUR OWN . . .

The billboard attacks on outsiders took many forms, some declaring that "no one except a low down scoundrel, a person lower than the dirtiest dog, yes, lower down than a skunk, would chew or smoke tobacco in Zion City." And during local elections the words were especially vehement. Billboards demanded that people

VOTE FOR GOD'S PARTY THE THEOCRATIC
PARTY.

As could be expected, residents who had no affiliation with the established church fought back with their own notices, demanding a right to live peacefully on their own property and to be able to vote as they saw fit. Billboards attacked the leader of the church, known as the General Overseer, by saying:

THE GENERAL OVERSEER DOES NOT OWN US—
WE ARE NOT HIS SHEEP. WHO IS HE TO TELL US
WHAT WE CAN SAY ON THE STREET, HOW TO
VOTE, HOW TO LIVE? THE GENERAL OVERSEER
IS A VICIOUS MAN LUSTING FOR POWER. LET
HIM TALK TO HIS SHEEP NOT TO US. WE LIVE IN
A FREE COUNTRY. WE ARE LAW-ABIDING CITI-
ZENS. SOMEONE SHOULD STOP THIS MAN WHO
RUNS OVER AT THE MOUTH AND PEN![46]

It took many years for the two different factions in Zion City to learn to live together without suspicion and hatred. As people from diverse religious backgrounds moved into the town, the established church lost its complete control of the city government. Government officials now represent varied religious groups, though predominantly Protestant groups. But the town government has resisted separation of church and state in its official emblems, as the court case over its religious symbols on government documents has shown. Zion's mayor has vowed to appeal that case to the Supreme Court.

A Democracy, Not a Theocracy. The Christian Catholic Apostolic Church of Zion was not the only community that attempted to establish a form of government based on religion. Along with the Puritans during colonial times and the Mormons later on, there have been many smaller groups.

Some of these groups, like the House of David in Michigan and the Oneida Community in New York, also were communes—people shared ownership of property and cooperated in the production of goods and services. Communal dining and community child care were part of such utopian religious communes as well. Although a few of these early religious communities have survived to this day, nearly all have changed their economic and social structures.

More recently, several extremist groups advocating theocracy have gained attention because of their militaristic and sometimes racist views. Among these groups is the Identity Church, which wants to see the U.S. government replaced by a theocratic republic for whites only. The Coalition on Revival (COR) also has a militaristic view and is committed to theocratic rule. The group has set up local armed militias prepared to battle against what it predicts will be an invasion by "communist Mexico." According to news reports, the COR has developed a manifesto that calls for training leaders in a "green beret boot camp" at its Kingdom College in San Jose, California. Other plans call for abolishing public schools, the Internal Revenue Service, and the Federal Reserve System. And the COR expects to set up a network of media to preach its ideas on the establishment of a "kingdom of God" on earth. [47]

Because of guarantees of religious liberty, people can exercise their right to live by theocratic doctrines, so long as they do not offend others or infringe others' rights. The

Bill of Rights protects people from intrusions on their beliefs whether by religious leaders who claim direct connections with God or by civil servants. Nevertheless, religious pressure groups still attempt through the political process to establish their doctrines as orthodox.

"Religious people involved in the political process must not make political issues into moral absolutes and moral absolutes into political issues," in the opinion of Robert Maddox, director of Americans United. He adds that "people must ever be vigilant in recognizing the unholy alliance between any brand of religion and any brand of politics . . . God does not belong to the United States. God is neither a Democrat nor a Republican. The healthiness of the political process suffers when one political party attempts to speak for God."[48]

Protecting
Religious
Liberties

The majority of Americans seldom think about government restrictions on their religious beliefs—they usually take their religious liberty for granted. But in some cases, Americans make a conscious effort to guard against restrictions on this important freedom. And some political leaders, civil rights groups, and religious organizations have supported or initiated legal action to protect religious freedoms.

Guarding Religious Freedom. Before individuals or groups can challenge laws or government actions that infringe religious liberties, they must establish "legal standing to sue." This piece of legalese means that plaintiffs (those who want to sue) must have a personal stake in the outcome of a debate in order to be heard by the court. It is not enough to object to a law or action on general principles. Federal justices decide whether plaintiffs have been threatened or injured or in some way adversely affected by a government action. If not, the case is dismissed for lack of standing.

Being able to show sufficient standing to initiate a lawsuit is no easy task and requires legal expertise. Plaintiffs in church-state issues (as well as in other civil rights disputes) often turn to national organizations that can help in such matters. These include the American Civil Liberties Union (ACLU), Americans for Religious Liberty, Americans United for Separation of Church and State, the American Jewish Congress, the legal action departments of various Christian and other religious groups, and national educational organizations.

Some American leaders have heaped criticism on some of these groups, particularly the ACLU. Public criticism of the ACLU usually stems from the fact that the organization tries to be impartial and has defended unpopular, even despised, individuals. Since 1920, the ACLU has defended the rights of individuals and groups whose free expression, due process, religious liberties, and other freedoms have been threatened or denied. As the ACLU's principal organizer, Roger N. Baldwin, once pointed out: "The test of the loyalty of the ACLU to its principles lies in the impartiality with which they are applied—there can be no favorites in defense of rights for all." The principles are especially difficult to apply when defending hated ideas and people.[49]

Another basic principle that the ACLU upholds is the concept of limiting or restricting the power of the majority. In cases where religious liberty is threatened, this may mean defending the rights of fringe groups like the Hare Krishnas or Scientologists, who have little political power and could easily be repressed. It also means taking legal action to protect the separation of church and state in highly controversial cases, such as those involving abortion, prayer in public schools, and tax funds for parochial schools.

The Anti-Defamation League (ADL) of B'nai B'rith also takes legal action in church-state issues, although its main purpose is to combat anti-Semitism and other forms of bigotry. As part of that agenda, the ADL maintains a civil rights division that through legal action confronts individuals or hate groups attempting to terrorize or discriminate against Jewish people. In addition, the organization develops and publishes a variety of educational materials to help churches, schools, and communities understand religious differences and the need to respect the nation's diversity.

Americans United for Separation of Church and State was established for the purpose described in its title. However, the organization was founded in 1947 as Protestants and Other Americans United for Separation of Church and State. Early members feared a "Catholic conspiracy," believing that Catholics were trying to take over the country. But today, the stated mission is to defend religious liberty for people of varied backgrounds, providing expert testimony for federal and state legislatures considering church-state issues. The organization also supports legal battles to keep church and state separate and publishes *Church & State*, a journal with news about church-state events, court cases, and attempts to restrict religious freedom.

Americans for Religious Liberty is another organization dedicated to the principle of separation of church and state. Its newsletter, *Voice of Reason*, edited by Edd Doerr, is designed to inform members about church-state issues around the globe. In addition, the organization works to counteract religious groups that threaten a woman's right to choose safe and legal abortions. Primarily, though, Americans for Religious Liberty attempts to educate the public about the real meaning of religious freedom, which goes well beyond being able to worship as one pleases. As

Doerr puts it, religious freedom means not only the right "to live one's life according to one's own beliefs, up to the point, of course, at which that free exercise of religion begins to interfere with the equal rights of another person." It also means the right "to make and follow one's own moral judgments and decisions of conscience on such matters as marriage and reproduction."

Doerr describes many more facets of religious freedom, but summarizes by pointing out that "the edifice of religious freedom . . . is one of the grandest and most magnificent ever erected. . . . We must never allow it to wobble, to crack, to erode, or to be destroyed."[50]

Respecting Religious Diversity. While national organizations attempt to guard our civil liberties, individuals, too, can be vigilant about threats to religious freedom. Perhaps one of the most important actions one can take is to learn to appreciate beliefs different from one's own and to eliminate bigoted attitudes. Many people are reared in families and live their lives within communities that share similar religious beliefs. If you are not exposed to other points of view or do not learn about religious doctrines other than your own, you are likely to be convinced that your beliefs, traditions, and values are absolute. This frequently leads to stereotyping and prejudice.

When people prejudge those different from themselves, they usually apply negative characteristics to all people in the "out" group. Some Christians, for example, may be convinced that Muslims as a group are warlike and that Islam is a religion of violence. But Islam teaches peace and love, and the fact that some Muslims may terrorize the world to avenge their grievances does not mean that Islam is a religion of terrorism.

If people hold prejudices—and almost everyone does—and act upon them, discrimination and physical violence may be the result, as has been true throughout human history. In addition, those who try to deny religious groups their freedoms, and sometimes even their lives, are likely to pass on their views to others. Parents, for example, teach their children prejudice through word and deed. Youngsters may learn at a very early age not to play with "them," meaning children who are labeled "different." Or children may hear religious groups labeled with derogatory terms like "Christ killers," "bead pullers," or "holy rollers."

But it is possible to undo some negative learning and to reduce prejudiced thinking when diverse religious groups have contact with one another. Suppose you want to find out about another person's religious belief. Why not engage in a thoughtful one-to-one discussion? You explain what you believe or don't believe, and the other person does likewise. The idea is not to change each other but to share thoughts and opinions.

In some communities, people learn about diverse religious beliefs by visiting each other's places of worship. A group of Mennonites, for example, might attend a meeting of Unitarian-Universalists, or Baptists might visit a Jewish temple. Historical museums and libraries are also sources of information about religious groups and people who have fought for the right to practice their religion.

Interfaith families also can be examples of how diverse religious views can come together, remain intact, and work in harmony. Candace Corson, a physician in northern Indiana, is an example.

Corson grew up in an interfaith home—her mother was from a Presbyterian background and her father from an Orthodox Jewish background in the Ukraine. She learned about the Christian belief in the resurrection of Jesus that is celebrated at Easter. She also learned that in Eastern Europe, Easter was the day of government-encouraged pogroms—Jews were killed because they were supposedly responsible for Christ's death. During her childhood, Corson celebrated the major religious holidays of both Christian and Jewish faiths and with her parents found "spiritual common ground" within the Quaker community.

Although she considers herself a Quaker, Corson passes on her interfaith heritage to her own children. But she says that does not mean mixing and diluting Christian or Jewish religious beliefs. In Corson's view each religion is true. "All religions have aspects of the divine" and it is important to see the truth in all religions and appreciate their worth, she says. "Religion is supposed to help people to be better human beings and to be kind to each other. All the major religions have a Golden Rule or a corollary thereof. If people would follow the basic teachings of the Golden Rule of their religion, we would have a better world. Instead, I see people using religion as an excuse why they shouldn't have to work together on the big problems facing humanity."[51]

A Basic Protection—The Bill of Rights. Being able to share beliefs and pass on an interfaith heritage is one of the benefits of religious freedom as guaranteed by the U.S. Constitution. To underscore the importance of that freedom, imagine what life might be like without it. Consider the possibility of living in a nation governed by members of a religious group called the Do-Gooders.

If you want to enjoy the "good life" and be respected by the majority, you would have to be a Do-Gooder. Like all Do-Gooders, you would be required to post a list of Do-Good rules in your home and read the rules aloud twice each day. The rules would require Do-Gooders to wear smile buttons to show that they were part of the religious order, and to prove their religious faith by living for one week a year in a tent in a national park.

No public dissent would be allowed in Do-Good land. All families would contribute part of their income toward the support of religious schools. All young people would have to attend Do-Good schools, including non–Do-Gooders, called Dunces. School classes would be held seven hours a day each day of the week. Dunces would have to sit on specially marked benches and wear cone-shaped hats to identify themselves. If you were a Do-Gooder, you would not be allowed to associate with Dunces, although you would be allowed to publicize their misdeeds. Probably, you would never learn about their values, which include protecting natural resources and respect for all living things.

Obviously, you could add any number of other hypothetical rules dictated by the governing Do-Gooders. But the point is, if a religious majority gains enough power, it can force its beliefs on others—unless pluralism and religious freedom are protected. Leo Pfeffer, a legal scholar and church-state expert, noted that our nation has shown the world "that a government whose concerns are purely secular and which leaves to the individual conscience of its citizenry all obligations that relate to God is the one which is actually the most friendly to religion. It is a precious jewel that we have. We should guard it well."[52]

Our form of government requires a constant balancing act to maintain government for the common good and at the same time to allow for individual freedoms. That balancing depends on the U.S. Constitution and those who uphold it. In 1991, Americans marked the two hundredth anniversary of the adoption of the Constitution's first ten amendments. The Bill of Rights has aged well. To assure its life far into the future, perhaps Americans should every now and then review those rights.

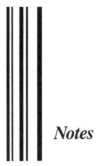

Notes

Chapter One

1. Glenn T. Miller, *Religious Liberty in America* (Philadelphia, PA: Westminster Press, 1976), p. 25.

Chapter Two

2. Samuel Eliot Morison, *The Oxford History of the American People* (New York: Oxford University Press, 1965), p. 272.
3. Quoted in Ravina Gelfand, *The Freedom of Religion in America* (Minneapolis, MN: Lerner Publications Company, 1969), p. 36.
4. *Ibid.*, p. 39.
5. David Little, "The Reformed Tradition and the First Amendment" in James E. Wood, Jr., ed., *The First Freedom* (Waco, TX: J.W. Dawson Institute of Church-State Studies, 1990), pp. 21–22.
6. *Thomas Jefferson: Writings* (New York: Literary Classics of the United States, 1984). Also quoted by H. Frank Way, *Liberty in the Balance: Current Issues in Civil Liberties* (New York: McGraw-Hill Book Company, 1981), p. 71.
7. Samuel Walker, *In Defense of American Liberties: A History of the ACLU* (Oxford and New York: Oxford University Press,

1990), p. 219. Also see Sidney H. Asch, *Civil Rights and Responsibilities* (New York: Arco Publishing, 1968), p. 44.

8. Delos B. McKown and Clifton B. Perry, "Religion, Separation, and Accommodation: A Recipe of Perfection?" (*Phi Kappa Phi Journal*, Winter 1988), p. 2.

9. William H. Rehnquist in a dissenting opinion in a 1985 school prayer case, *Wallace* v. *Jaffree*.

10. Albert Erlebacher, "The Flowering of Religious Liberty" (*Chicago Tribune*, Perspective Section, January 27, 1990), p. 10.

11. Norman Redlich, "Religious Liberty," in *Our Endangered Rights* (New York: Pantheon Books, 1984), p. 261.

Chapter Three

12. Quoted by Sidney H. Asch, *Civil Rights and Responsibilities* (New York: Arco Publishing Company, 1968), p. 50. See also Don Lawson, *Landmark Supreme Court Cases* (Hillside, NJ: Enslow Publishers, 1987), p. 94.

13. Religious News Service, "Mandatory Pledge to Flag Was Outlawed in 1943" (*Los Angeles Times*, Metro Section, September 10, 1988), p. 7.

14. Stephen Scott, *Why Do They Dress That Way?* (Intercourse, PA: Good Books, 1986), pp. 6–8.

15. John A. Hostetler, *Amish Society* (Baltimore, MD: John Hopkins Press, 1968), pp. 194–195.

16. *Ibid.*, p. 199.

17. Quoted by John D. McCallum, *The Encyclopedia of World Boxing Champions* (Radnor, PA: Chilton Book Company, 1975), p. 73.

18. Marla Donato, "Dozens Find Out How to Refuse to Fight War" (*Chicago Tribune*, January 27, 1991), p. 3. Also see Associated Press bulletin, "Reservists Seek to Be Objectors in Face of War" (*Los Angeles Times*, January 29, 1991), section A p. 11; Ruth Rosen, "Two Women Draw a Line of Their Own" (*Los Angeles Times*, December 20, 1990), section B p. 7; Mary McGrath, "4 West Coast Churches Offer Help to Soldiers Who Refuse to Fight" (*Philadelphia Inquirer*, January 6, 1991), section A p. 10; and Amy S. Rosenberg, Andrew

Maykuth, and John Woestendiek, "Hundreds in U.S. Search for Way Out of Military" (*Philadelphia Inquirer*, January 18, 1991), section A p. 15.

19. Quoted in "Sales of Church Materials Ruled Taxable" (*Chicago Tribune*, January 18, 1990), p. 3. Also see David G. Savage, "Supreme Court Upholds Sales Tax on Church" (*Los Angeles Times*, January 18, 1990), section A p. 3.

20. Quoted in "Court Invalidates Tax Break for Bibles" (*The Washington Post*, May 13, 1990), section A p. 7.

Chapter Four

21. Quoted by Lorenzo P. Romero, "Court Rules That 'Minister' Must Abide by Medical Law" (*San Jose Mercury News*, June 30, 1989), section B p. 2.

22. Glenn T. Miller, *Religious Liberty in America* (Philadelphia, PA: Westminster Press, 1976), p. 113.

23. Jim Robbin, "Utah Lawsuit Tests Mormon Power" (*Chicago Tribune*, October 21, 1990), News Section, p. 2.

24. William E. Moody, "Christian Science and Child Health" (*Newsday*, July 24, 1990), p. 49. Also see Curtis J. Sitomer, "Prayer and the Public Trust" (*The Christian Science Monitor*, February 28, 1990), pp. 10–11; Joan Connell, "Christian Science vs. Medical Science" (*San Jose Mercury News*, November 19, 1988), section D p. 1; Doris Sue Wong, "SJC Rules on Right to Refuse Care" (*Boston Globe*, January 16, 1991), p. 27.

25. Quoted by Nat Hentoff, "A Blow to Freedom of Religion" (*The Progressive*, December 1990), p. 16.

26. Ethan Bronner, "Court's Curb on Religion Draws Fire" (*Boston Globe*, January 6, 1991), p. 2.

27. Stephen J. Solarz, "The Court's Erosion of Religious Freedom" (*Newsday*, February 14, 1991), p. 71.

Chapter Five

28. David Fellman, "Religion, the State, and the Public University," in James E. Wood, Jr., *Religion, the State and Education* (Waco, TX: Baylor University Press, 1984), pp. 70–73.

29. Glenn T. Miller, *Religious Liberty in America* (Philadelphia, PA: Westminster Press, 1976), p. 110.

30. As quoted by A. James Reichley, *Religion in American Public Life* (Washington, D.C.: The Brookings Institution, 1985), pp. 137–139.

31. Norman Dorsen, ed., *Our Endangered Rights* (New York: Pantheon Books, 1984), pp. 261–263. Also see Samuel Walker, *In Defense of American Liberties: A History of the ACLU* (Oxford and New York: Oxford University Press, 1990), pp. 224–225; H. Frank Way, *Liberty in the Balance: Current Issues in Civil Liberties* (New York: McGraw-Hill Book Company, 1981), pp. 74–76.

32. Phone interview. Also see Edd Doerr, "Does Religion Belong in Our Public Schools?" (*USA Today*, September 1987), pp. 48–50.

33. Richard P. McBrien, *Caesar's Coin: Religion and Politics in America* (New York: Macmillan Publishing Company, 1987), p. 180.

34. "Religion in the Public School Curriculum: Questions and Answers" (undated pamphlet).

35. "Alexander: No Tax Aid for 'Weird' Schools?" (*Church & State*, April 1991), p. 14.

Chapter Six

36. Garry Wills, *Under God: Religion and American Politics* (New York and London: Simon & Schuster, 1990), pp. 16–17.

37. Quoted in Alan R. Ball and Frances Millard, *Pressure Politics in Industrial Societies* (Atlantic Highlands, NJ: Humanities Press International, 1987), p. 203.

38. Geoffrey Parrinder, ed., *World Religions from Ancient History to the Present* (New York: Facts on File Publications, 1983), p. 507.

39. *Ibid.*, 226. Also see "Polish Clericalism Resurfaces," (*Voice of Reason*, Winter 1991), p. 11.

40. Albert J. Raboteau, "Kin and the Tradition of Black Religious Protest," in *Religion and the Life of the Nation*, Rowland A. Sherrill, ed. (Urbana and Chicago: University of Illinois Press, 1990), p. 54.

41. Martha Minow and Aviam Soifer, "Abortion and Religious Liberty" (*Chicago Tribune*, May 18, 1989), p. 23.
42. Quoted in William Grady, "City Seals Ruled Unconstitutional" (*Chicago Tribune*, March 20, 1991), p. 1.
43. Jonathan D. Sarna, "The Problem of Christmas and the 'National Faith,' " in *Religion and the Life of the Nation*, Rowland A. Sherrill, ed. (Urbana and Chicago: University of Illinois Press, 1990), p. 163.
44. Poll conducted by ICR Survey Research for the Associated Press from November 16 to November 20, 1990.
45. Richard G. Hutcheson, Jr., *God in the White House* (New York: Macmillan Publishing Company, 1988), pp. 203–206.

Chapter Seven

46. Author's collection of news accounts and church papers from the period.
47. Fred Clarkson, "Wildmon Kingdom?" (*Mother Jones*, November/December 1990), p. 11. Also see People for the American Way, *Right Wing Watch*, January 1991, p. 2.
48. Robert L. Maddox, *Separation of Church and State* (New York, The Crossroad Publishing Company, 1987), pp. 190–191.

Chapter Eight

49. Quoted by Norman Dorsen, ed., in the introduction to *Our Endangered Rights* (New York: Pantheon Books, 1983), p. xiv.
50. Edd Doerr, *What Religious Freedom Means* (pamphlet published by Americans for Religious Liberty, 1990).
51. Phone interview.
52. Earl Raab, ed., *Religious Conflict in America* (New York: Anchor Books, 1964), p. 163.

 *Further Reading*

American Civil Liberties Union. *Our Endangered Rights*, ed. by Norman Dorsen. New York: Pantheon Books, 1984.

Fowler, Robert Booth. *Religion and Politics in America*. Metuchen, NJ, and London: The American Theological Library Association and The Scarecrow Press, 1985.

Gelfand, Ravina. *The Freedom of Religion in America*. Minneapolis, MN: Lerner Publications Company, 1969.

Hunter, James Davison, and Os Guinness, ed. *Articles of Faith, Articles of Peace*. Washington, D.C.: The Brookings Institution, 1990.

Hutcheson, Richard G., Jr. *God in the White House*. New York: Macmillan Publishing Company, 1988.

Kleeberg, Irene Cumming, and Richard Brandon Morris. *Separation of Church and State*. New York: Franklin Watts, 1986.

Lawson, Don. *Landmark Supreme Court Cases*. Hillside, NJ: Enslow Publishers, 1987.

Levy, Leonard W., ed. *Encyclopedia of the American Constitution*. New York: Macmillan Publishing Company, 1986.

Maddox, Robert L. *Separation of Church and State*. New York: The Crossroad Publishing Company, 1987.

McBrien, Richard P. *Caesar's Coin: Religion and Politics in America*. New York: Macmillan Publishing Company, 1987.

Menendez, Albert J., and Edd Doerr, eds. *The Great Quotations on Religious Freedom*. Silver Spring, MD: Centerline Press, 1991.

Reichley, A. James. *Religion in American Public Life*. Washington, D.C.: The Brookings Institution, 1985.

Walker, Samuel. *In Defense of American Liberties: A History of the ACLU*. New York: Oxford University Press, 1990.

Way, H. Frank. *Liberty in the Balance*. New York and Toronto: McGraw-Hill, 1981.

Wills, Gary. *Under God: Religion and American Politics*. New York: Simon & Schuster, 1990.

Wood, James E., Jr. *The First Freedom: Religion & The Bill of Rights*. Waco, TX: J.W. Dawson Institute of Church-State Studies, 1990.

Index

Gandhi, Mohandas K., 84
Gobitis case (1940), 34
Graduation prayers, 70, 72
Gulf War, 42–43, 102

Hare Krishnas, 48
Henry, Patrick, 21, 22, 23
Hickey, Jim, 99
Hinduism, 73
Holiday displays, 97–98
Homosexuality, 92, 99
House of David, 107
Hughes, John, 63
Humanism, 73
Hussein, Saddam, 42
Hutterites, 36

Identity Church, 107
Interfaith families, 113–114
Iran, 84, *85*
Islam, 57, 84, 102, 112
Islamic Society, 102

Jackson, Robert, 34
James I, king of England, 15
Jefferson, Thomas, 23, 24, 26,
    62, 82
Jehovah's Witnesses, 32, *33*,
    34, 53
Jews, 19, 65, 87, 91, 94, 111
Judaism, 57, 73, 97, 98

Kennedy, John F., 100
Khomeini, Ayatollah
    Ruhollah, 84, *85*
Killea, Lucy, 94
King, Martin Luther, Jr., 89,
    91
Ku Klux Klan (KKK), 60, 62,
    87, 89, *90*

Last, Stephen, 101

Lee v. *Weisman* (1991), 72
Legislative prayers, 28
Liberal religious groups, 92
Liberty University, 45
Lutherans, 80

Maddox, Robèrt, 35, 108
Madison, James, 23–25
Maher, Leo T., 94
Malone, Dudley, 77
Maryland Toleration Act of
    1649, 18
Mayhew, Bridget Mergens,
    59–60
McBrien, Richard P., 78
*Memorial and Remonstrance
    against Religious
    Assessments* (Madison), 24
Mennonites, 32, 36, 39
Menorah, 12, 98
Methodists, 65
Military service, 13, 39, 40,
    41, 42
Mohammed, 84
Moral Majority, *71*
Mormons (Church of Jesus
    Christ of Latter-day Saints),
    49, *50*, 51–52, 65
Morton, Thomas, 16

National Association for the
    Advancement of Colored
    People (NAACP), 89
National Association of
    Christian Educators, 70
National Conference of
    Catholic Bishops, 92
National Council of Churches,
    87
National Interreligious Service
    Board for Conscientious
    Objectors, 43